Learner Driver on the Road

BRENDA CAREY

Copyright © 2024 Brenda Carey

All rights reserved.

The author asserts the moral right to be identified as the author of this work. No parts of this publication may be reproduced, stored in a retrieval system or transmitted, in any form or by any means, electronic, mechanical, photocopying, recording or otherwise, without the prior permission of the publisher. Where appropriate, the names of individuals mentioned in this publication have been changed to protect their identities.

Some information contained in this book has been obtained from GOV.UK and is reproduced in accordance with the Open Government Licence version 3.0. For details of the licence please refer to https://www.nationalarchives.gov.uk/doc/open-government-licence/version/3/.

Book cover by Simon Carey.

Published by Maddocks House Publishers

Available from Amazon.UK

ISBN 978-1-7384157-0-0

CONTENTS

Chapter One – Who'd be a driving instructor	1
Chapter Two – Now the real thing	21
Chapter three – Unusual situations	53
Chapter Four – Other drivers	72
Chapter Five – You can't please people all the time	84
Chapter Six – Near and actual accidents	102
Chapter Seven – Breakdowns	123
Chapter Eight – Manoeuvres	132
Chapter Nine – Incidents at the test centre	140
Chapter Ten – The driving test – Theory and Practical	153
Chapter Eleven – Dreams	176
Chapter Twelve – Petrol stations	180
Chapter Thirteen – Animals	186
Chapter Fourteen – The last chapter	194
Anecdotes	199

DEDICATION

Dedicated to all my pupils who I had the pleasure of teaching. It was a challenging but also a pleasurable adventure. May your good driving skills be worthy to others.

ACKNOWLEDGEMENTS

To all those who gave help and advice and heartened me when writing this book. To my husband for being my fourth emergency service and my answering machine before mobile 'phones. To my son for designing the book cover and my daughter
for her encouragement.

Welcome to the zany world of a driving instructor.

This book is not just for learner drivers but also for those who can drive and anyone thinking about becoming a driving instructor.

Brenda takes you into the world of driving instruction and speaks about her most unforgettable pupils. Not only will you read about the unbelievable things that can happen when teaching someone to drive, but also the craziness of other drivers on the road.

The book contains hilarious couldn't-make-it-up stories, facts and advice.

Lord Leslie Hore-Belisha said, "Driving is an art in which those who are engaged should, in the interest of their own and of the public's safety, take the greatest pains to make themselves proficient."

CHAPTER ONE

WHO'D BE A DRIVING INSTRUCTOR

Thirty-six years of driving instruction taught me a greater understanding of people. Laughing so much that your belly hurts and crying with happiness when someone with disabilities passes their driving test against all odds. So many people have said to me,

"How can you do *that* job? Are you mad?"

"You must be a nervous wreck by the end of the day."

"I wouldn't have the patience to do *that* job. So how do you cope with it?"

"Thirty-six years as an instructor! Haven't you topped yourself yet?"

"I feel sorry for you because you can't watch the telly in the evening, and you're missing out on the soaps!"

Gosh, I was missing out on the soaps! How different my life would have been if I had been at home to watch them. However, I could do and did *that* job because I felt I was helping people change their lives. Most people, especially the 17-year-olds, just wanted to learn to drive. Others desperately needed a driving licence to gain independence, get that dream job, move house or leave home. Sometimes a few craved, when they were upset, a listening ear with them not driving and me acting as their psychologist! Then, the very nervous and older people who had postponed learning to drive for most of their lives. They eventually took the plunge, not believing they were sitting in the driving seat and those with disabilities. Lastly, the cocky ones who knew it all, anyway!

It has been a roller-coaster of laughter, sadness, crying, dread, surprise and other incredulous happenings. I have met many interesting people, from all walks of life wanting to learn. It has been a privilege to help others succeed, even if, as you will discover in this book, some paths are bumpier than others.

So why did I want to become a driving instructor? It may have all started when my Dad took me to collect his new car when I was three. I watched him give a man sixpence (6d old money), and he sat me in the back seat, got in the front and drove us home. In my innocence, I thought he had bought the car for 6d. Later in life, reminiscing with Dad about it, we laughed.

"If only," he said. "I was paying the man 6d to rent a garage he owned to keep the car safe, and this was the first payment."

Before Dad bought the car, we travelled around on my parents' tandem bike. They attached a sidecar to it for Judy, the dog, and me to sit. So, why did my Dad decide to buy a car? I do not know. Perhaps my Mum wanted a more comfortable way of travelling with a child and a dog.

The car was a black 1950s Singer four-door saloon. Dad kept it in the rented garage, still using the bus for work. The car only came out on high days and holidays. As I got older and we went out for a ride, I would ask questions and intently watch how he operated the pedals and steering wheel. Also, I pointed out the road signs to him and told him off if he went too fast. I was a typical back seat driver! The car is still special to me because it was the first car I drove when I was thirteen. It was on private land, up and down my auntie's flower nursery. When we arrived at my auntie's house, I could hear them talking.

"She'll be OK. Nothing to worry about," said Dad.

"I don't mind if she gets behind the wheel, but be careful of my greenhouses," she replied.

Then he looked at me and said, "Come on then."

"Where are we going?" I asked.

"You are going to drive my car. It'll be OK. Just have a go."

"Wow!" I excitedly shouted, jumping up and down.

He laughed and said, "Don't get too excited. We don't want you crashing!"

We got in the car, and I had to sit on a cushion to be able to see over the steering wheel. It was a long driveway, so I could practise starting, stopping, and changing the gears. So, thinking about it, my Dad must have been courageous and my auntie incredibly trusting, as there were five big greenhouses along the way. Still, I did not hit any of them!

I also remember a day when we were heading to my auntie's house, and my Dad had a minor accident. I was very young and cannot remember how it happened, but I recall looking out the rear window to see a black line on the road behind us. I kept telling Dad about it, but he initially ignored me.

"What are you going on about?" he asked, finally fed up with my persistence.

"There's a black line on the road behind us," I persisted. "But there isn't one in front."

Sighing, Dad pulled over to the side of the road and got out to investigate. When he got back in, his chagrin was apparent.

"OK, OK, the petrol tank is leaking, so we'll have to turn around to go home," Dad said. "You were right. I should've listened to you earlier."

I like to think that I was honing my observation skills even then.

So, when I was 17, I immediately applied for my provisional licence and took my test in 1966. The cost of each lesson was 17 shillings and 6d (roughly worth £15.42 at the time of writing). The cost of my driving test was £1 and 15 shillings (approximately worth £30.83 at the time of writing). I learnt to drive in a Ford Anglia with a yellow bottom and a white top. I loved driving the car and, to this day, have always wanted to own one. Well, maybe one day! On the day of my test, which was 9 am on a chilly January morning, my instructor, Mr Potts, came to pick me up. I was a nervous wreck. I got in the car, started the engine, got into first gear, and tried to find the 'biting point'. I say *tried* because I could not find it at first, bringing the pedal up too far and stalling, then not bringing it up far enough, so the car did not move and the engine raced. When I finally found the biting point, I could not take the handbrake off as it was so stiff. I was near to tears and had not even moved off yet.

"Calm down," Mr Potts said. "You'll only make it worse by getting yourself in a state."

"But you've done something to this car," I snapped.

"Don't be so silly," he retaliated.

Mr Potts was a lovely man in his 50s and laid back. He and his wife owned the local hardware shop; while she ran the shop, Mr Potts was out teaching people to drive.

Finally, I got moving and drove towards the test centre. On the way, he asked me to park on a steep hill to practise the 'hill start'. But I could not do it. I kept rolling back, and this time was in tears.

"It's just your nerves," he said, keeping himself calm.

Eventually, I moved the car without rolling back, and then it was time to go to the test centre. When we got there and sat in the waiting room with the other three candidates, it was not long before my driving examiner came in and called my name. We had parked the car in a designated area within the bus station. As we approached the car, the examiner stopped me so I could read another car's number plate, which I read wrongly. He asked me to read another one, but I got it wrong again. However, this time I realised I did not have my glasses on. I had taken them off in the test centre and forgotten to put them back on again. He gave me another chance to read another plate when I put them on, and thank goodness I read it correctly.

FACT – You should be able to read a number plate (with glasses or contact lenses if necessary) at a distance of 20 metres (or 20.5 metres for old-style number plates). The allowance is three attempts. If you get it wrong on the second attempt, the examiner will measure the exact length, and if it is

incorrect again, you will fail your test. (At the time of writing).

We then got into the car, and I turned on the engine and somehow moved away, but the examiner started writing things down, and I thought I had failed already. However, I gradually felt my nerves disappear. I got on with my driving, even managing a hill start without rolling back, and I did not stall. When we returned to the car park, he asked me the first of three questions on the Highway Code.

"How do you turn right off a motorway?" he asked.

"You can't," I replied, confused.

"Well, how would you do it?" he asked again abruptly.

It clicked, and I explained what you would do.

"Come off at the next available exit and turn right at the top," I said, looking at him to see if there was a glimmer of hope in his face that I had got the question right. There was none, just carrying on to ask the other two questions.

He told me I had passed. I was in shock and could not believe it. Mr Potts was waiting near the car, and when the examiner got out, he came over. I got out of the car and started jumping up and down.

"I've passed! I've passed!" I shouted at him.

"I know. I could see the examiner filling out the pass sheet," he said calmly.

Driving home, he said apprehensively, "I have a confession to make."

"What do you mean?" I queried.

"Well, the car you used in your lessons broke down this morning, so you were driving a different car," he said anxiously.

"What!" I shouted and then started shaking.

He looked at me and said, "Look at you. That's why I didn't say anything."

"Well, that explains why I couldn't do the clutch and the handbrake. I knew it felt different but couldn't understand why; now I know!"

Luckily, Mr Potts had another exact Ford Anglia, the same yellow bottom and white top, so I could not tell the difference. It looked the same until I tried to get the biting point, stalling and rolling back on the hill start. Cars were unreliable in those days, so he had another car, just in case, and I was extremely grateful. Otherwise, no test!

"I'm very proud of you for passing the first time. Just goes to show you've been able to cope under pressure," Mr Potts said with satisfaction.

When I got home, my Dad's friend was there, and he gave me a Mars bar to celebrate! That Mars bar tasted so good, and I forgave Mr Potts.

After passing my test, I was excited and keen to get out on the road, but I did not have my own car and wanted to use my Dad's. However, he had different ideas and told me his insurance policy did not cover my driving unattended. As he had only just renewed the policy, it would be another year before I could drive alone. I believed him but learnt later it was a ruse, saying he just wanted me to practice more before I was let loose with his car. The first time he sat with me, he was exceptionally nervous and went white as a ghost as I drove. I do not know why, as I thought I was pretty good! After a few more times out on the road, he became more relaxed, and we did a big drive to my auntie's flower nursery, about 72 miles away.

After the year was up, my Dad gave me the freedom of his car. However, I had a few mishaps, so perhaps it was a good idea not to allow me to drive his car straight after I had passed. I backed into a stationary vehicle, broke the rear cluster lights, and got a parking ticket within a few weeks of being on the road. On another occasion, I drove to my boyfriend's house (who is now my husband). While waiting at a busy roundabout to turn right, I was in the left-hand lane and knew I was in the wrong road position. I was looking through the car's side window to the right, so when it was clear, I moved off, but I had not checked the front and went straight into the back of a Mini Minor. Four boys got out of the Mini and came over to me. You can imagine how I felt as the four of them approached me. However, the driver was kind to me, and we exchanged details. It probably helped both cars were still roadworthy.

I got to my boyfriend's house and telephoned my Dad, who was, thankfully, relatively undisturbed by it. Another time, while in a petrol station, which was not self-service, the attendant told the woman in front of me to reverse so he could get the petrol hose to reach the fuel tank. Still, instead of looking behind her to see if it was clear, she reversed and hit me. Well, at least this time, it was not my fault, but my boyfriend, looking at cars through the showroom window, thought I had driven into her.

"What've you done now?" he shouted.

"I didn't do anything. It's the attendant's fault and the woman's for not looking out of the back before reversing," I retorted.

However, the big accident was when somehow I bent the exhaust pipe on my Dad's new car. I did not tell him what happened, but I think it was when reversing onto a high kerb. Unfortunately, the exhaust became noisy, and the car was only six months old, so he could not understand why the exhaust was going so soon. Then, when travelling along a seamlessly long winding country lane, the exhaust broke in half and dragged along the road with sparks flying out of it. I was only 19 and scared, but I did not want to stop; I just wanted to get home. The car behind me kept hooting, but there was no way I was stopping, and I dragged the broken exhaust for the rest of the journey home. It is a wonder my Dad still allowed me to use his car, but he did.

Years later, I got married and had children. When they reached school age, my husband asked what I wanted to do. I saw an advert in the local newspaper about becoming a driving instructor a couple of years before my daughter started school. So, I cut out the article and wrapped it around a paintbrush, of all things! The more I thought about it, the more it appealed to me. So when my husband asked, I went to get the paintbrush (I think he thought I wanted to become a decorator!), unwrapped it and showed him the newspaper cutting. It surprised him because I had not mentioned it before but said if it was what I wanted to do, go for it. I had been at home with my children for eight years and was a secretary before then. However, new technology brought in word processors and computers. The only advanced technology I had used before giving up work was an electric typewriter, which meant possibly going back to college to train.

Meanwhile, I had been typing documents for a friend's husband at home. When deciding to see about training to become a driving instructor, the company I worked for asked if I would go into their office for a few weeks. They wanted me to cover for one of their secretaries while she was on holiday. Luckily, they still had electric typewriters! I was excited about working in London again, but not travelling. It was winter, and they cancelled the trains because of bad weather, mainly snow. It brought back memories of standing shivering on the platform, waiting for a train that would not come. Nothing had changed!

After covering for one of their secretaries for two weeks, the company offered me a permanent secretarial position. Still, by now, I had got in touch with the driving school offering the training and had an interview with them. I explained I had been working from home, typing documents, and the company had offered me a permanent secretarial position in their office. I was in a quandary about what to do, as I needed a job to pay for my training. The person interviewing me asked if I could type some documents for him, which I did. They then offered me a secretarial position in the driving school's office, including my training. So how could I refuse?

I started working for the school, but they overlooked my training. We had a few differences of opinion about it as my boss wanted me to stay in the office. He would go across the country, training people to become driving instructors. So, when he set up a training session in our local area, he could not refuse me to be on the course with six other trainees. It was 1984, and you had to take three tests (you still do) to become a Driving Standards Agency - (DSA) Approved Driving Instructor - (ADI). Nowadays, it is called the Driver and Vehicle Standards Agency - (DVSA).

The three tests involved a theory test with 100 questions and two practical tests. The practical tests involved a driving test lasting one hour leading straight into an hour's instructional test. They are now separated, so a candidate will take the driving test one day and the instructional test another day. When I learnt to drive, Mr Potts, my instructor, did not need any qualifications. However, in 1962, a voluntary register became active under the Road and Traffic Act. Still, taking the driving instructor exams was unnecessary until 1970, when official registration of all driving instructors was required.

The theory was the first test to be taken and passed before the practical tests, and it was down to me to study for it. The way to get anything into my head is to write it down and record it on a tape recorder. What is a tape recorder? Well, they are still about! I rewrote the Highway Code about five times and the Driving Manual the same. When I felt ready to take the theory test, I had to go to London to sit it, and I passed the first time.

For the practical side, we would have our lessons, then practise with each other or get friends and family members to act as our pupils. I used to practise with Marion and Trevor, who were also on the course. On one occasion, I asked my Mum to help. Now she was not a confident driver, and it was a wonder she ever took her driving test, seeing as she used to hold the handrail when my Dad was driving. However, she did and passed the second time, and we were v-e-r-r-y proud of her. Marion was with me, and we arranged a lesson on teaching my Mum how to do the turn-in-the-road (commonly known as the three-point-turn, now no longer in the driving test). Marion went first, explaining the procedure. Although my Mum had to do this manoeuvre on her driving test, she got herself into a state and undoubtedly put Marion through her paces. After my turn, we drove Mum home, and then on the way to my house for Marion to pick up her car, we talked about how it had gone.

"Your Mum is such a talented actress," she gushed.

I burst out laughing and said, "Marion, she wasn't acting. It's how she is! I knew she would be an excellent candidate for us. She doesn't really like driving and only drives locally and for convenience. It was good for her to be taught again. You did a good job with her."

Mum, bless her, and Dad came out quite a few times to help me.

I was pleased to pass my theory test for the first time, but the practical tests were a different kettle of fish. You must have a car with dual controls for the tests, and my boss said I could borrow the driving school car. However, the day before my tests, he called me to say I could not have the car as he needed to go somewhere. I felt devastated, and we had a big argument, with my husband taking the telephone from me to talk to him. Things calmed down when my husband had the idea of him using our car and me having the school car, and my boss agreed. He brought the school car around the following morning, but it was filthy dirty as usual. Luckily, my tests were in the afternoon, so I cleaned the car inside and out. Then, as I was relaxing in the bath, the telephone rang, so I had to get out of the bath to answer it; it was my boss. I was unhappy with him, although he had telephoned to wish me good luck. Guilty conscience, I thought.

It was time for me to leave, and I had to drive to Epping, about 20 miles away. As I left my house, the heavens opened, and it started raining heavily, and I thought I had better practice the emergency stop, which I did a few times. Happy with that, I started my journey to the test centre. On the way, a lorry approached me and sprayed mud onto my windscreen and over the bonnet. I pulled the lever to wash and wipe the windscreen, but there was no water in the windscreen washer bottle, so I drove into a garage to clean the car as best I could and fill up the bottle. I arrived at the test centre feeling distraught but calmed down while waiting for the examiner.

Eventually, my examiner appeared, and we went out to the car. After my eyesight test, we got in the car (this time, I was wearing contact lenses), and we set off for my driving test. The test included three manoeuvres. One was reversing around a corner to the right, which I needed to improve and was worried about. So when my examiner asked me to park on the left so he could explain that he wanted me to do the reverse corner to the right, my nerves kicked in, and making matters worse, near the corner was a stationary Bedford van. I felt I needed more room to come in behind it; also, I had restricted observation. I told him so, but he was not interested and told me to get on with it. Well, with also needing more confidence with this manoeuvre, it was double trouble. Still, I thought it was fair to middling. Then we came to a junction where I was extremely hesitant. It felt like six years had passed before I got the car moving. My brain told me to go, but my feet were not obeying my brain.

I finished my driving test, and we swapped seats for the instructional exam, where my examiner became my pupil. It was hard to put him in that context because you had to act as though he knew nothing, but he knew everything. There were three sections: a novice learner, a mid-way learner and a learner at test standard. I got through the novice learner section, and we parked for the next session. He wanted me to teach him how to take left-hand and right-hand junctions. I explained what to do and told him to drive on when he was ready. He drove off without looking in his mirrors or doing a blind spot check. I turned round quickly to ensure we were safe, blinked, and my contact lens fell out of one of my eyes into my lap. That put me in an overly anxious state. I asked him to park on the left and mumbled that my contact lens had fallen out and I needed to put it back in my eye. After I sorted it out, I told him to drive on, but horrors of horrors, I forgot to tell him what he had yet to do. He was also cutting a right corner, for which I had to grab the steering wheel to get him back to the left. I asked him to pull over on the left to explain how bad it was not to check correctly before moving away and how dangerous it was to cut a right corner. However, it sounded gibberish, and, of course, the explanation came too late.

After completing stage three of the practical test, which went reasonably well, we again swapped seats, and I had to drive him back to the test centre. This was still part of my driving test.

Then, you were not informed if you had passed or failed (you immediately know nowadays), and I had to wait for two weeks, but I knew I had messed up. Marion passed the month before and said to come to her house to tell her about it. When she opened her front door, I was sobbing on her doorstep because of all the tension I had built up with what had happened the previous day, driving to and on the test and knowing I had failed. I could not stop and sobbed when I tried to speak to my husband over the telephone. Finally, I calmed down enough to drive home. Still, when my husband opened the front door, I sobbed again, but he hugged me and told me not to worry.

"Just do it again," he said, calming me down. "You know you can. It's given you the experience, so work on that."

"OK," I sobbed. "You're right."

When I got to work the next day, my boss asked how I got on. What did I say to him? I'll leave that to you to decide.

As expected, I had failed my driving test on the reverse corner to the right and for being hesitant at the junction. I also failed in the instructional part of the second section for not advising the examiner on observation before moving away and cutting the right-hand corner. Well, I knew that already!

My boss was an excellent trainer but got into severe debt when working away. He did not pay his bills for hiring hotel conference rooms and did not pay for advertising in newspapers. The bailiffs were after him, and I knew I had to pass my practical test before they put him out of business. So I booked my next test and had to convince myself I could pass by standing in front of a mirror and telling myself I could do it. However, the bailiffs had caught up with him, and the business had to be closed. Fortunately, Marion had started her driving school and said I could hire her car for the test.

So, the day arrived for my second test, which was in the morning. I drove to her house and picked up the car. When I reached the test centre (nothing had happened on the way), I sat in the waiting room then my examiner came out. It was a different one, and his name was Mr Bean. Well, having a test with Mr Bean (Rowan Atkinson, the comedian) strapped into a seat sitting on top of the car as in one of his comedy scripts would have been fun. But Mr Bean and his antics still needed to be on television and would not appear for some years.

He was a genial man and made me feel relaxed. Unfortunately, on my driving test, we went to the same junction where I had been hesitant and guess what? I was again, but not so bad this time. However, my right reverse corner went off like a dream. I nearly went down on the third section of the instructional test, but Mr Bean stopped me and reminded me it was the test standard stage. So after the test finished, I drove back to Marion's house. She opened the front door, and I said if I had not passed, then they wanted blood.

It was Christmas, and I had to wait five weeks before my result came through instead of the two-week wait. I repeatedly reviewed the tests during that time, constantly questioning myself. Then the post arrived, and the envelope was on the floor. I knew I had passed because it was a thin envelope, unlike the bulky one which had come before.

Oh boy, I was so relieved. I could now start my business, and the year was 1985. As I did not want to work for a franchise company, I looked for a suitable car, settling on a 1980s Mazda 323 saloon. Unfortunately, money was short, so as my husband had a company van, we sold our private car to buy the Mazda. The car was the first in my name, so I did not have car insurance. Fortunately, my husband's insurance company allowed no claims bonuses to be transferable to their spouse's insurance. Which is what we did to lower my insurance cost.

Before becoming a driving instructor, the first person I accompanied to a driving test was my husband (then my boyfriend). He could drive but had yet to take his driving test. I nagged him about it, and he booked a test. In those days, the test included arm signals, but I could not remember how or when this came into the test.

"Just do the arm signals all the time," I suggested. "The examiner will tell you when to stop," not believing what I was saying.

"You sure?" he asked apprehensively.

"Yes, it should be OK. I think that's what I did on my test," I doubtfully replied.

"Alright, I'll see how it goes," he said, looking worried.

My husband used his car for the test, a Ford Consul, but the brakes needed attention. So, he 'bled the brakes' the day before his test and mended the windscreen wipers, which fought each other in the middle of the windscreen! They were vacuum wipers, so the faster you drove, the slower the wipers would wipe! The day arrived. It was a good job he had sorted the brakes and windscreen wipers because it was pouring heavily with rain. His examiner was about 6 foot 6 inches tall and just as wide (or was I imagining it?), and out they went. While driving, my husband opened his window, practising the indicators and arm signals together. The rain was still coming down in torrents and into the car, so he was getting soaking wet. The examiner asked him to park up on the left and explained he wanted him to 'stop the car in an emergency' and showed him the signal he would use when to stop the car. Now, remember my husband had bled the brakes the day before, and we did not wear seat belts.

FACT – The law requiring seat belts was enforced on 31st January 1983. Then in 1991, the law changed again, making adults wear seatbelts in the back of cars.

They drove on. From the corner of my husband's eye, he saw the examiner lift his clipboard and lean forward to hit the dashboard. Seeing as the examiner was already beginning to lean forward and my husband was performing the stop simultaneously, the poor man landed up in a heap on the dashboard!

After the examiner gathered himself, he said, "I won't be asking you to do *that* again. Drive on when you are ready."

Then, as they approached a T-junction, the examiner was not directing him.

"Which way do you want me to go?" my husband asked.

"I beg your pardon," the examiner snapped.

My husband looked to his right and saw a 'No Entry' sign. Whoops!

After all that happened, my husband thought he had failed the test. He was getting wet and fed up, so he wound the window up and drove as usual; at least the windscreen wipers were still working! On the way back to the test centre, the examiner did not seem interested in his driving as he looked elsewhere. Arriving at the test centre, it was time for the Highway Code questions, but the examiner first said,

"There was no need to give all those arm signals. Were you trying to pull the wool over my eyes?"

"No," answered my husband. "I thought that's what you had to do!"

"Well, it isn't. I would have told you when and where," the examiner retorted.

He then asked him twelve Highway Code questions when typically it was only three or four! One question my husband questioned *him* on. The examiner replied, "I'm asking you, don't ask me." We have often wondered if the examiner was being hilariously offensive by asking my husband all these questions and seeing him get soaking wet. Was he getting his own back because he threw him onto the windscreen when executing the emergency stop? However, he answered the question correctly as he had learnt the Highway Code inside out and got every question correct. That satisfied the examiner, and he passed him. He told him he would let his young lady know he had passed. Hey, that was me! When he came into the waiting room, he told me he had passed and laughed.

It was still raining, and my husband was pulling the 'L' plates off the car when I got outside. We grabbed each other and started jumping up and down, laughing. A man sitting in his car behind us was laughing as well. We got into the Consul and went to go, but he promptly stalled the engine, which made us laugh more, and the man in his car behind was clapping his hands. Still, we do not know how he passed, but he had shown the examiner he could drive safely and, of course, knew his Highway Code.

Eventually, when I knew what I was doing, I taught my son, daughter and three nieces to drive. I also trained one of my nieces to become a DVSA Approved Driving Instructor, but then she went over to the dark side and became an examiner!

CHAPTER TWO

NOW THE REAL THING

An anecdote from one of my pupils…

"You're only allowed to drive at 29 ½ mph."

Starting a business can be daunting and take a long time to establish. I advertised in the local newspaper, with no response. In contrast, Marion and Trevor had done so in their area and got a lot of interest and pupils. Instead, I had leaflets printed, which my family and I posted through letterboxes in my area. As a newcomer, I offered a discount, and I got a reaction. This upset some of the established instructors in the neighbourhood because I had a few rude telephone calls. One day I was at the test centre with a pupil and joined the conversation with other instructors after the pupils had left for their tests. A lady instructor was complaining about the new instructors' discounts. Was she one of the unhappy instructors? My parents vaguely knew her, and I asked if she remembered them. She ignored me, then looked at the instructor sitting next to me and said,

"Is she one of your pupils?"

"No," he said, looking wary and turning to me.

"Actually, I am one of those new instructors discounting," I piped up.

She looked daggers at me, got up and walked out of the waiting room. The other instructors laughed and said, "Ignore her. She's always moaning about something."

Then, lessons were about £5 per hour, and tests were much cheaper than they are now. I had my first telephone call from a lad enquiring about lessons. I booked him in for a Sunday morning and did not know who was more nervous. He did not realise he was my first pupil and was happy at the end of his lesson and eventually passed his test for the first time.

Gradually, my book increased. Then a lady in her early thirties telephoned for lessons. She acted slightly neurotically and did not have any coordination. When you learn to drive, you use hand and eye coordination and hand and feet coordination, but she had neither. In her first lesson, I knew I had my work cut out. She was all over the place, totally uncoordinated and with no common sense. Thank goodness I had dual controls and, mercifully, seat belts, so at least she did not throw us through the front windscreen when she slammed on the brakes.

"You know, Audrey, you don't have to brake so hard. The car will stop even if you are lighter with the footbrake, and we won't get seatbelt burn or whiplash. I have explained this to you before and shown you," I said, trying to reassure her and rubbing my neck simultaneously.

"But I'm so scared that the car won't stop in time," she answered.

"It will if you brake gently to slow the car beforehand as you travel to the spot where you want to stop. Then just a little more pressure to stop the car and slightly ease the pressure before you stop. I know it isn't easy when first learning to drive because the clutch has to go down just before you stop to prevent the car from stalling. Your right leg will want to follow your left leg, but your right leg must stay lighter on the footbrake. Let's practise this again," I said. "Remember, it is called progressive braking."

So setting targets ahead of us, we continued practising for the next hour, but to no avail. It took another four months of driving around the block to practice the controls, especially the footbrake, before I dared to go out on the main road. Audrey began having two double lessons per week, which did help, but it took two years before I could put her in for a driving test. Finally, it came to her fourth attempt; it was summer, and a 4.15 pm test was booked. In those days, the DVSA added extra time to the day because of the lighter evenings, finishing around 4.45 pm.

By this time, she had got into essential oils and brought along a bottle of oils to help calm her. I did not know she had this until she began throwing it around in my car without my permission, after which my car stank. She then sprinkled some onto a handkerchief and breathed it in. Sitting in the waiting room, she kept breathing in from her handkerchief, and I mean breathing in, taking intense breaths. I was worried she would pass out. When the candidates had gone for their tests (she had one of the friendly examiners), the other instructors looked at me and said,

"Is she alright, your lady? Looks like she's in a right old state."

"Yes, she is. I thought she would pass out, breathing in the essential oils she sprinkled into her handkerchief. She's also flung it around in my car without asking me."

They all laughed, saying, "Been a bit of a challenge, has she?"

"You could say that," I replied with a sigh.

Then, after the test, instructors had to wait until the examiner got out of the car. So I was expecting him to be out at around 4.50 pm. It was hilarious watching him trying to escape. Door opening, one leg out, another leg out, and it was not until 5.15 pm that he fled altogether. She had told him her entire life history. He came over to me, apologising for taking so long and saying she could talk a hind leg off a donkey and wanted to know why the car smelt like it did. I told him what had happened, thinking it would calm her. Maybe her strategy was correct because she passed.

I had another lady similar to my previous pupil (I was her third instructor). Still, I did not take her to test standard as she could not cope and kept making excuses to finish her lessons earlier than she had booked with me. The last straw came when she booked a two-hour lesson and told me she needed to cut the lesson short to go shopping. Well, I had had enough. It appeared shopping was more important than learning to drive. So I charged her the entire time, whereas stupidly before, I was lenient. I did not see her again after that.

So, although I was in a comfort zone of teaching, I realised that teaching some people to drive could be challenging. As others think, you do not just sit on your backside all day, enjoying the ride. However, now and again, you begin lessons with someone and immediately know they will be a doddle. They are above-average learners and have the gift of driving.

One girl, a friend of my daughter, sticks in my mind. It was as though she had been born to drive, and I only had to give one explanation of a subject, and she did it. She learnt quickly and passed minus faults when I gave her a mock test. She then passed her real driving test with a clean marking sheet. After her test, as she and the examiner walked across the car park, I could hear them talking.

"But I must have had some faults," she said.

"No." the examiner replied. "Look, a clean sheet."

"I don't believe you," she protested.

"What's the matter?" I asked as they reached me.

"He says I don't have any faults on my test sheet. But I must have made some," she said, still protesting.

I looked at the sheet, and it was clear.

"Claire," I said enthusiastically. "You have passed with no faults. You clever girl."

"Really!" she exclaimed.

She looked at the examiner and apologised for not believing him. He laughed and said it had been a pleasure to be her examiner. As the years went by, many pupils passed without faults, which made me feel good, knowing I must be doing something right.

Unfortunately, some people who find the theory and practical tests easy do not understand why others take much longer to learn and/or keep failing. They do not appreciate they are among the few lucky ones, as most are average learners. You can be highly academic and pass the theory test with flying colours. Still, you must have the practical skills required to pass the practical test, which some do not. A non-academic person can find it hard to pass the theory test but has the practical skills to drive a car. They may have taken their theory test five times but passed their driving test the first time.

In contrast, others need help passing the theory and the practical tests but carry on. I admire them for their determination to succeed. Then there are the very nervous people who may have taken a while deciding to learn to drive (even those in their sixties) and have made the brave decision to do so. Sometimes it was necessary, or they have become fed up with relying on public transport or other life-changing reasons. Also, there were those with disabilities. Although they found it challenging to drive, after passing the practical test, they were over the moon.

I had a girl who was a basketball player playing for her school team and a woman who played basketball for the county. They both had good hand and eye coordination but not hand and feet. Neither could understand why they found learning to drive difficult. They took a reasonable time to learn, one passing the first time and the other the third time.

One of my older ladies said, "Brenda, can you tell me why I can make my legs and feet walk forwards and backwards but not make them go up and down on the pedals?"

"Well, perhaps you need to give them a good talking to. Tell your brain to let them know they are part of your body," I jokingly replied, to which we both burst out laughing. Glad to say she passed on her second attempt.

A girl I was teaching was having trouble with the steering, and I really could not understand why, as I had explained and shown her. Then, one day, I asked her to take a junction and heard her counting.

"What are you doing, Sally?" I asked.

"Counting how many times I turn the steering wheel," she replied.

"Why are you doing that?" I queried. "I've not told you to do that."

"Oh, but my mum said it was a good idea."

"Did she now!" I exclaimed.

No wonder we were having trouble, which had been going on for about ten lessons. So, although I had shown and explained how to steer the car, she took her mum's advice and counted the wheel turns. So I went through it with her again and, 'voila', she could now steer properly.

I did a dual carriageway lesson with one of my girls. I got her to do 70 mph because it was safe to do so, and on a driving test, if you can, and it is called for, you need to show the examiner that you can do the speed. Making progress. When she got home and told her mum, she was angry and said,

"What does Brenda think she's doing? You are a learner driver and can only drive at 29½ mph."

When she came for her next lesson, she told me what her mum had said. So, I asked her where her mum had got 29½ mph from.

"She could've said no more than 30 mph," I said, trying to keep a straight face.

"Well, I don't know. I expect my mum is worried I might have an accident if I go too fast," she replied.

"You could have an accident on a dual carriageway or motorway if you unnecessarily drove at 30 mph, where a car's speed limit is 70 mph. So isn't it better for you to learn with me to drive on a dual carriageway and drive at 70 mph if it's safe? Remember, you might have to do this on your driving test," I consoled.

"I suppose so, but will you please explain it to my mum? She won't believe me," she shyly replied.

So after her lesson, I spoke to her mum and said it was part of her learning and not to worry. I had another girl who would not drive at 70 mph on the dual carriageway because she did not like it. As previously mentioned, if you make progress, it could prevent you from failing. Incredulously, she failed her test because she had made too much progress! Driving along the dual carriageway, she broke the speed limit by driving at 80 mph to overtake a vehicle. She was upset and said I told her to do it! Er, I don't think so. It would be best to get on with it, but you should not break the speed limit. So, if it means you will, you stay behind the vehicle, driving at the appropriate limit for that occasion.

Another girl, when shown the road work sign for a lane closure with two lines and a half line, answered that you could only drive at 11½ mph! I really could not keep a straight face on that one.

One of my scariest lessons (and I have had a few!) was in the Great Storm of 1987. The evening forecast on 15th

October 1987 referred to strong winds, but heavy rain would be a significant problem. The Met Office also warned the emergency services about the bad weather.

On the 16th October 1987, I picked up one of my pupils. It was raining and windy, but nothing to suggest what was to come. However, her one-hour lesson turned into three hours. Realising the weather was getting worse, and a storm was brewing, we finished the lesson to return home.

We were only three miles from her house, but the storm worsened. Cars broke down, and people panicked, running for cover. We followed a diversion into a small estate as trees had fallen, blocking other roads. It was a nightmare because all traffic, including heavy lorries and buses, became diverted. It took us three hours to get through the estate because the lorries and buses had to deal with parked vehicles, sharp ends of roads and turnings. After I dropped her off, I had to get home. That took another two hours. There were no mobiles then, so I had to wait to call my other pupils from my house telephone. Of course, they all knew I would not be taking them out. I also rang poor, suffering Bridget to make sure she was alright.

"No need to worry," she said. "I felt exhausted, but I enjoyed it. It's given me more confidence to learn to drive, and I'm really looking forward to my next lesson. Of course, Mum and Dad were worried about us, but I did OK, didn't I?" she asked excitedly.

"You sure did, Bridget, and I can see you will make a skilled driver. See you next week for your lesson." Had it been another person, it may have had the opposite effect.

Apparently, a woman had telephoned the BBC to say she had heard a hurricane was coming. However, Michael Fish, the weather forecaster in 1987, denied it and has never lived it down.

On another occasion with a different pupil, we had to deal with diverted traffic along the single-track road because of a road blockage. A bus was coming towards us, and there were no passing places. We stopped, and so did the bus. Well, we both had to! There were vehicles behind us and behind the bus. The only way to get past the bus was to go up onto a sloping grass verge at the side of the road!

"Would you like to have a go, Ruth?" I asked.

"Are you kidding?" she said, looking at me as if I was bonkers.

"Well, I needed to ask you. What if you had been on your own?" I queried.

"I will never drive down country lanes when I pass my test. NOT EVER!" was the emphatic reply.

So, that told me!

We swapped seats, and the bus driver got out of the bus to direct me through. I was just as scared as anybody else, as we were at an acute angle, hoping the car would not turn over. To our relief, we got through. We swapped seats again, and the road widened slightly, but Ruth still had to negotiate through the oncoming traffic. She did it brilliantly but reiterated she would never drive along a country lane again. I bet she did!

In 1999, the DVSA introduced the Pass Plus scheme, and a few of my pupils took it up after passing their driving test.

FACT – The Pass Plus Scheme comprises six modules, taking no less than six hours to complete. All modules are practice-based, but some may have to be theory. There is no test at the end, just an evaluation of Achieved or Exceeded. If a module has to be theory-based, the result would be Achieved. At the time of writing, the modules are:-

- **Town driving. I would take my pupils to a town where they have not driven before.**
- **Driving in all weathers. Although sometimes, this had to be theory-based because of the weather.**
- **Rural road driving. Practising on different routes.**
- **Night driving. It may have had to be theory-based because of the time of the year.**
- **Driving on a dual carriageway. Using a different dual carriageway.**
- **Motorway Driving. Depending on where you lived, to what motorway you would use.**
- **However, in June 2018, learner drivers could drive on motorways. The condition was that they were with a driving instructor, thought competent enough, and the car fitted with dual controls.**

One Pass Plus lesson I remember remarkably well. After passing her test, one of my girls, Wendy, wanted to take it. We went through the modules, and the last thing was to tackle the motorways. We would use the A1 (M) and the M25. Then if there was time, we would take the M3.

However, it turned into a horrendous lesson, raining at first but culminating in a storm. We had a lorry in front, behind and next to us. We felt trapped! The rain hit us from all angles, and the windscreen wipers could not cope.

"I don't like this. In fact, I HATE IT!" Wendy exclaimed forcefully, revealing her exasperation.

"I'm not too keen either, but it's a great experience for you. In the future, when you drive along a motorway, it will be a breeze," I said, looking at Wendy with a smile of encouragement.

"I think I would get my Dad to come with me if I drove on a motorway again," she replied.

"I don't blame you," I said. "The good thing is, it hasn't put you off."

The traffic was going oh-so-slowly, and we had passed the last junction before the M3, so we had no choice but to carry on. We were into two hours of her three-hour driving lesson and would usually have been on the way back home. We reached the M3. It was a brief run, and we could turn around to go home at the end. The storm passed, but we still had to be careful of flooding on the motorways and the spray of other traffic. Two hours later, we arrived at her house. Her parents were frantic because we could not telephone them. Again, no mobile. We were both dog-tired, but she definitely had the experience of what could happen on a motorway. I do not think she will ever forget that lesson.

I would deliver lessons, no matter how I was feeling health-wise. It was a hot summer (well, some of it!), and I had been working in the garden most of the day before. We had moved to a new location, but I still taught pupils in my old area until they had passed their tests. I did not want to let them down. I started the drive down to Nick's house, and halfway there, I started feeling ill, but I carried on and got to his house. By this time, I felt sick and had a nasty headache. I took some headache pills and told him it would pass, so we carried on with his lesson and drove to the test centre about 12 miles away. It did not give, and I felt progressively sick. Luckily, it was time to go home, and I realised I had sunstroke from working in the garden the previous day. I warned Nick that if I asked him to pull over in a safe place, he should do so as soon as possible. On the way home, I knew I would throw up at any moment, and pleased there was an area for us to pull over. I got out of the car and was sick. Can you imagine what the passing drivers must have thought? Perhaps:

"Poor woman, that must have been a terrible lesson."

"Wouldn't like to be in the car with him."

"That must have been a bumpy ride."

Poor Nick drove back to his house, the best I had seen him drive, which shows how, if pushed, you can cope in an unpleasant situation. So I called it a day, went to my son's flat where I was staying, cancelled my following lessons and slept for the rest of the day.

Out on a lesson, we heard police sirens behind us, and I was preparing Julie, my pupil, to pull over to the left to let the police pass. Little did we know we were involved in a police chase. It was a good job that I had taught Julie how to emergency stop because as we were pulling over, the car being chased overtook, skidded in front of us and stopped. A young lad jumped out of his car and ran for it. His girlfriend was in the front passenger seat, crying. Then the police car also overtook and pulled up directly in front of us, with inches to spare between us. The police then jumped out of their car to chase the lad. Julie was so shaken up that she started crying. I had to console her and joked about how exciting it was; it was something she could, in the future, tell her grandchildren. Then she could not stop talking about it.

The son of a close friend who was learning to drive with another instructor (I couldn't teach him as he lived too far away) was on his driving test. Going through the town, and this is the absolute truth, a bank robbery occurred. The men jumped into the getaway car and pulled out before him. He had to emergency brake!

He calmly asked the examiner, "Shall we chase the getaway car?"

The examiner laughingly said, "We could try. It would make an interesting test. However, I hate to spoil the fun, but I think you should carry on with the test when you're ready."

What excitement in a driving lesson and test, being involved in a police chase and a bank robbery!

I taught a lady named Pauline, who was in her middle sixties. Now she was not what most people would think of a woman in her sixties, as she was determined, fun-loving, and could turn her hand to most things. For instance, her daughter was arranging her car insurance when she got her car, and the insurance broker wanted to speak to Pauline. However, her daughter had to apologise and said Pauline could not come to the telephone as she was on the shed roof repairing it! After being widowed for a couple of years, Pauline set about accomplishing things her husband would not have allowed her to do. She went to college and took a City & Guilds course to become a masseur, and passed, then wanted to learn to drive.

She would have me in stitches telling me what she got up to, but on one occasion, when she told me about driving at 3 am on her own, I scolded her and told her not to do it again.

"Well," she said, "I couldn't sleep!"

"I don't care if you could or could not sleep; you don't take the car out alone in the middle of the night. Don't you realise that's when the police are about more looking for drivers breaking the speed limits and doing other stuff?"

"I wasn't speeding," she replied sheepishly.

"Promise me you won't do it again, or you'll lose your provisional licence before you get your full one," I said in annoyance.

"Oh, alright, I won't," she huffed.

Then, in one early-morning lesson, we approached a mini-roundabout. Children were going to school, and one schoolboy walked out in front of us across the roundabout. Mercifully, we were already slowing down, but as he went across the roundabout, he gave us the two-finger salute behind his back. Pauline showed anger by leaning towards the windscreen and giving him the one-finger salute.

"There, you didn't expect that! Did you!" she exclaimed.

The look on the boy's face was a picture.

Well, what can I say? Again, as a professional, I should have told her off, but this time it doubled me up with laughter.

A memorable Mancunian lady, Colleen, whom I taught to drive, also used to have me in stitches with how she acted and what she said. When I first saw her, I thought she looked tough, and I had better keep her on the right side of me, but she was one of the kindest and funniest people I have known. She had tried to learn to drive before but was unsuccessful. Her coordination was terrible, and she was unbelievably nervous but determined to learn. In addition, she wanted to improve her lifestyle as she had been through the mill when she was younger. Altogether it took about two-and-a-half years for her to pass.

She did not have a clue about the perception of space, speed or distance, and teaching her to deal with approaching the end of the road would have my hair standing on end. I would tell her to slow down with the footbrake, change gear, and stop at the end of the road. But she would stare ahead of her and speed up! Trying to teach her the manoeuvres (it was then only the reverse corner and turn-in-the-road) was also a nightmare. It took months for her to grasp the idea of manoeuvring.

She married, had moved from Manchester, and just had a baby. When her husband could not babysit, we took the baby out with us, strapped her in, and she would fall asleep. Sometimes, Colleen got despondent and thought about giving up. Still, I would remind her about her ambition and that it would happen. At long last, she was more than test-ready, but she doubted whether she would pass, and I had to build her confidence. She failed the first test, but it did not put her off. She booked the second test, and for the week after, she had booked a holiday to Spain. While learning, she worked her way up to be a manager of a Women's Refuge. This also involved travelling to different places, so she needed her licence. When I picked her up for her second test, she had a different demeanour and was eager to take the test. I knew she was going to pass, and she did. She said she had to pass because she did not want to go on holiday to Spain unhappy. Good for her!

What made me laugh was when I stopped beside her husband's car while he was waiting for her to come out of work one day. The baby was sitting on his lap and excited when she saw me.

Laughing, he said, "It comes to something when even the baby knows the driving instructor." Then jokingly added, "I expect you will be off to the Bahamas with the amount of money she's spent learning to drive!"

"Oh, ha-ha, I said. "I know it's taking a while, but she'll get there. You should be proud of her for carrying on when she finds it difficult."

"Yeah, I am. Because I really didn't think she'd keep it up. So, only joking."

"She's a determined lady," I replied.

Later I taught Colleen's son to drive, and later still started to teach the baby we used to take with us, who was now a lovely 17-year-old girl. Sadly, though, she did not want to learn. She was not ready for it, but hopefully, she bit the bullet and became a driver as she got older. Speaking of which, you must want to learn to drive, or you will not enjoy your lessons, which will become challenging. So do not let people bully you into it. It is not worth the effort.

I have had a few occasions where babies and children would come out on driving lessons. Every weekend, a man I taught had his baby and would bring her with him. Older children would enjoy the ride or fall asleep, others would read their books or play on handheld devices, and some we could not take with us because they were too boisterous.

As well as Colleen's daughter, not all people want to learn to drive. You also might think that all men and young lads have the instinct to do so, but that is not necessarily the case. Some men and young lads have no inclination to drive and/or feel nervous about learning. Their family or friends may have pushed them into it, as in one man I started teaching. He said his family kept on at him about learning to drive, but he was uncomfortable with it. Then when some teenagers saw him in a learner's car and taunted him, he felt embarrassed and gave up, which was sad. I have also taught a few women to drive whose husbands refused to think of the idea. They have tried to talk them into it, but in the end, they have taken up the gauntlet.

When teaching an exceptionally nervous 45-year-old man (who wanted to learn), we practised hill starts and catching the clutch on one particular lesson. He got himself in a terrible state and sweating badly. I showed him the procedures several times, but I had to give up on it, as I feared he would stop learning altogether. When we got home to his house, his wife opened the front door. She frowned at me with a 'what's been going on' expression. I had to get out of the car and explain what had happened. Usually, I would let the pupil know what we would tackle the following week when the lesson ended. Apparently, when he got home from the last lesson, he told her we would practise hill starts and catching the clutch in the next lesson. He was not looking forward to it, and it was all he could think about; therefore, he had a brain block. The good thing is we got to grips with it in a later lesson, and he passed his test the first time. A few years later, I taught his two sons to drive.

The next exceptionally nervous pupil was a girl I taught. She amazed her parents and me with what she did after passing her test. While learning, she would sit in the driver's seat, gripping the steering wheel tightly and with her nose nearly touching the windscreen.

"Madeline, you don't have to sit with your nose on the windscreen. Try to relax; it will make you feel better," I reassured her.

"I can't relax. I'm scared!" she exclaimed. "What if I crash the car?" she asked.

"No, you won't crash the car. Remember, I have dual controls and will prevent you from crashing," I answered reassuringly.

"Promise?" she queried.

"Yep, I promise," I said.

After a few more lessons, her courageous mum asked if she could take her driving in the family car. I warned her about her nervousness and said to only take her on quiet roads. Perhaps early on a Sunday morning. Gradually she settled down in her seat, not holding the steering wheel so tightly, with her nose coming progressively off the windscreen and beginning to enjoy learning to drive. She had a two-hour lesson with me every week and eventually drove her mum to go shopping and other places. Her confidence grew, and after passing the theory test, she booked her practical test. However, we were told that the examiner was unavailable when we arrived at the test centre, so her test could not proceed. It was upsetting, but we could do nothing about it. She booked a new date, continued with lessons and drove with her mum. She passed the first time with flying colours.

When she was learning, she taught international students English. The students would arrive in the UK and spend a few weeks learning English. After a while, she became headhunted and asked if she would take a position in a French school to teach English to the children. She accepted and went to live in France, where she had to drive to a school in the French Alps! So now she was in France, driving on the right-hand side of the road, in the snow, up the Alps. When her mum told me what she was doing, I was gobsmacked. She later lived in Italy and drove there.

Another very nervous pupil I taught went on to take the Emergency Response Driving Training course (ERDT) for their job. So, both being very nervous learner drivers, one going on to drive up the French Alps and the other taking the ERDT course (both risky situations) says something about achievement.

I have had pupils be physically sick on their way to their driving tests. When I went to pick her up, one woman looked white as a sheet when she opened her front door and felt really ill. "I can't do this test," she proclaimed. "I've been sick four times this morning."

"Oh, Barbara," I said. "Come on, you know you can do it. I'll sit in the back to give you moral support. You're absolutely ready for this test."

"*Will* you sit in the back?" she questioned me earnestly.

"Of course I will," I answered.

By the time we got to the test centre, she had calmed down, got her nerve back and passed the first time.

"There you are. I knew you could do it," I happily said.

"I honestly didn't think I could," she replied. "I'm so going to party tonight."

The thing to remember is that there are no perfect drivers. We all make silly mistakes, like stalling the car maybe once or twice, crunching the gears, and slightly rolling back on a hill start. Driving for too long in second gear when you could have been in third or not putting the button in when applying the handbrake, which I hate. It is such an irritating sound and not good for the care of the handbrake. I would say 'button in' when my pupils forgot the button, and they would soon remember it. Suppose you make a mistake like the above on your driving test, but it was not detrimental. In that case, the examiners may sometimes class it as finesses or not worthy. However, if you keep making the same driver mistake (also known as a minor mistake), you might fail by having three or more marks in one box, as you would for one serious mistake.

A mother whose daughter Sarah had dyspraxia telephoned me. People suffering from dyspraxia can find learning to drive difficult because it can affect their coordination. We had a long chat, and I explained it could take a long time for her to master the car's controls and that maybe it would be better if she learnt in an automatic car. But her mum said she wanted to drive a manual car, and it did not matter how long it took. It took three years.

First, I had to get her able to use the car's controls, putting the car into gear and balancing the clutch and accelerator together to find the biting point. Then learning to coordinate the steering and change the gears and the feet, working the footbrake, gas and clutch. Subsequently, it was checking the mirrors and blind spot-checking. Gradually she became more and more coordinated, but we had a lot of highs and lows. After getting the coordination reasonably sorted, we tackled general junctions. Then roundabouts, which can be everyone's weakness. She grasped the concept of going left and ahead at roundabouts, but turning right or full circle did not come easily. I showed her by demonstrating it, drawing diagrams and using a toy car. After many hours, she finally got the idea.

Just to add, there have been a few occasions when I have asked other pupils to go straight ahead at a roundabout; they literally try to go straight over it. They also try to turn right immediately when asked to take the exit to the right of the roundabout.

Then it was onto the two manoeuvres, as mentioned before. The turn-in-the-road Sarah grasped reasonably well, but the reverse corner was hard. We practised and practised, and finally, the idea was coming. Her mum asked if she could go on a driving lesson with us to see how she was getting on. Sarah showed her how she was accomplishing the reverse corner and did it exceptionally well. Her mum was over the moon, saying she could do it better than herself. We were all in happy tears at how she was grasping the idea. After all the above, she had to learn to read the road, hazard percept, and control the car independently, which can take a while for anybody learning to drive.

Meanwhile, her mum had bought her a car, the same make and model as mine, and asked if I would teach using her car. So, I agreed to take the bull by the horns, but there were no dual controls! We started lessons in her car, and she was getting on well locally, but then it was time to go further afield with those pesky roundabouts. One mini-roundabout sticks in my mind. As we were approaching it, she was not slowing down soon enough.

"Sarah, slow down. Sarah, start braking. Change down the gear," I urgently and fearfully said, trying not to shriek at her.

There was no response, so I *had* to shout at her, which I hated to do, but this time, it needed to be done as I had no footbrake.

She finally started braking but still travelled at 20 mph, approaching the roundabout on a bridge. I quickly had to intervene with the steering wheel so we could go over the roundabout, which, thankfully, was not a raised one, clear of traffic, and not crash off the bridge. Was my heart in my mouth? The answer is a big YES! Of course, it shook her up as well, but in some respects, it was good because it made her much more aware of being the sole driver of the car and had her and my life in her hands.

"I'm so sorry," she said, nearly in tears. "I could've killed us."

"Well, you didn't," I said in utter shock. "But it's taught you a lesson that you must always concentrate and be aware of situations when driving."

She passed her theory and practical tests for the first time. Her mum, friends, neighbours, and I were oh-soooo proud of her. Later, after she passed, I was at a roundabout, in the left-hand lane, ready to turn left, and she came on my right-hand side to turn right. We waved to each other, and then she was off before I was. The satisfaction of seeing her on the road, confidently driving, and turning right, was brilliant.

I taught a couple of friends of hers who had learning disabilities. Although learning took them a while, they succeeded and became independent. However, unfortunately, speaking to another friend's parents, I could see it was unlikely that she would cope with driving. They understood and said to give it ten lessons and see how it goes, but sadly it was not to be.

I started teaching Sadie to drive after her sister, Mary, began learning with me. Sadie suffered from Spina Bifida and was an exceptionally determined girl who would not let her disability hamper her from how she wanted to live. She did not want to learn in an adapted car, although she had one leg slightly shorter than the other.

"I can do this," she said. "I won't let my disability get in the way. I know my leg will hurt for a while, but I will get used to it."

"I admire you, Sadie," I said. "You know it will take a while, but if you've got the patience and determination, I'm sure you will succeed."

Her right leg was shorter, and that leg was for the gas and footbrake. She would have her seat as far forward as it would go, and although it was a strain at first, she did not let it get her down, and her leg grew stronger as time passed. Dare I say she was a better driver than her sister? She passed her test the first time, and her sister Mary succeeded on the second attempt. Again, it gave me great satisfaction to have played a part in Sadie's life to become independent.

Tina, who I was teaching to drive, worked in a residential centre for autistic people. A resident, Josh, knew she was learning and kept asking if he could have a go. So she asked me and explained that his disability did not stop him from learning new things, but he could find it challenging. However, as he was enthusiastic about it, he would be raring to go. So, we arranged a date and time, and she would come with us. I went to collect them, and he was so excited.

He sat in the front passenger seat, and Tina was in the back. As I was driving to a private area I had got permission from the owner to use, I explained things to him, and he watched me intently. Arriving at the site, we then swapped seats and bit by bit, I got him driving. The site's layout was like a road system with 'T' junctions, left and right corners, and 'roads' long enough to get him up to third gear. By the end of the two-hour session, he could, by my guidance, use all the car's controls, albeit haphazardly, which made him ecstatic. Josh felt exhausted at the end of his lesson but pleased with himself, and Tina was so happy with him. When Tina had her next lesson with me, she said that Josh had not stopped talking about it, and anybody who did not know soon did! Bless him.

Family competition can start, especially when teaching husbands, wives and siblings. I started teaching a lady to drive, and a little while into her lessons, her husband began learning. You can imagine their rivalry. When my lady passed her test the first time, the pressure was enormous on her husband to pass. He was over 6 feet tall and had to double himself up to get into my car and lever himself out.

So, with great relief, he passed the first time, as did their son a few years later. One happy family.

Similarly, when teaching twins or brothers and sisters to drive, there is competitiveness between them and a lot of banter. However, teaching identical twin boys was a pleasure. They learnt at an equal pace, having their tests booked on the same day, one in the morning and the other in the afternoon. (They wanted to take their tests consecutively). However, on the day the first twin to take his test had a telephone call cancelling it because of unforeseen circumstances. When I went to pick David up, he told me what had happened. I advised their mother to ring the booking office to determine if Sam's test was going ahead. It was not, and the booking office were not at all helpful. However, she refused to leave it there, kept telephoning, and somehow spoke to a supervisor. Finally, she succeeded in getting their tests re-booked for the following week, again consecutively. They had the same examiner, and both passed the first time.

I had my work cut out when teaching non-identical twin boys. Their personalities were completely different. They were each given money for their 18th birthday, and both decided to use it to learn to drive. One was determined and concentrated on learning, passing his test the first time. His twin, however, had a negative attitude. He blamed me for not learning as quickly as his brother. Not accepting that it would take him longer to learn because of his ability. I praised him when he finally achieved a goal, but he argued with me when he did something wrong. It got to the point when I had to drop him after he started cancelling or being late for lessons.

I taught twin girls who, although identical, had individual personalities. Monica was the least confident of the two and constantly compared herself to April, her sister. I had to put a lot of work into building up her confidence. Both took the same time to learn but had their test on separate days. Monica went first, and she passed, and the confident one, April, who could take more pressure, took hers the next day and passed.

Teaching a twin boy and girl was completely different, the boy being confident and quick to learn, but not his sister. He was always taking the mickey out of her, and I expect she had to suffer a lot of teasing at home. Both passed the first time, with a time gap between their tests.

Penny, who I taught to drive, took a while to learn as she had coordination problems and was a little reckless. She had been with me for a year and a half and kept asking when she could take her test.

"You're not ready for your test yet; you need more practice," I said when she asked me again.

"OK, I'll ask my husband to take me out," she said.

When I saw her for the next lesson, I asked if he had agreed to help her.

"No, he didn't and said he would not take me out in a million years. I thought it was unkind of him to say that. I won't tell you what I said to him," Penny answered.

"Oh, dear," I replied. "We'll just have to carry on as we are."

"Ah, but my father-in-law said he would take me out in his car," she gleefully said.

"That's great, but get him to take you out on quiet roads first so he gets used to your driving."

When I saw her for the next lesson, I asked how she got on.

"Well, I thought we were going along the road nicely, but we came to a bend, and I didn't slow down enough and took it too fast," she said shamefacedly. "Father-in-law was extremely uptight and said I took the bend like *shit off a stick!*"

We both cracked up at his description.

"Is he going to take you out again?" I asked apprehensively.

"Would you believe it, yes!" she exclaimed.

"Well, maybe that little fiasco has been good for you, making you realise how fast you are going for the conditions, as I have repeatedly told you," I replied.

Her driving improved considerably with the extra practice, and we decided it was time for her to take her test.

While on the lesson before her test, I asked her to take the left turn off the one-way system we were driving along. She was not reacting to my directions, so I repeated the request. As she was still not preparing for the turn, I thought she would miss it and carry on the one-way system. But no, just as we were about to pass the junction, she twigged what I had said. She suddenly swung the car to the left, where a man was standing on the centre island watching this car come hurtling towards him. I took the steering wheel and started braking, and we missed him by inches.

"*P e n n y,*" I screamed. "What the hell was that?"

"I'm so sorry. I was thinking about the test and not concentrating," she declared.

"You can't do that. You have got to be focused all the time. So I don't think you should take this test. You're too shaken up," I replied in exasperation.

"Please, let me do the test," she pleaded.

It took a little while for me to decide, then said, "OK, you can take the test, but I'm going to put a bag over my head so the examiner doesn't recognise me. And you'd better pay attention to your actions so you don't kill yourself and the examiner! And bring my car back undamaged!"

She went out on her test, but I didn't think she would pass, but to my amazement, she did! I could not believe it, and when we got home, her husband was waiting on the pavement for her. When he was told she had passed, the look on his face was of total disbelief, and he called the examiner a few names. After her test, she still had lessons with me to get her more roadworthy, and in the last lesson, I gave her some advice.

"You're to drive on your own for six months before you even contemplate taking the children out, and then only one at a time until you feel confident to take them together," I demanded.

"Alright, I'll do as you say," she replied.

After about a year, I bumped into her (excuse the pun) in the supermarket.

"How's it going?" I enquired. "Had any mishaps?"

"Only one," she said. "I was out with the children, and they were arguing in the back seat. So, I turned round to tell them off, and when I looked back at the road, we were heading for a lamppost, and I went straight into it."

"Oh my goodness, was anyone hurt?" I asked.

"No, thankfully, but it taught me a big lesson," she ruefully replied.

"I did what you said about not going out with them until at least six months after I passed and only one at a time. This was their first time together, so now I know what to do in the future; ignore them."

"Yes, definitely," I replied. "Thank goodness there were no injuries to any of you."

I used to see her now and again, and she had settled into her driving. I eventually taught her daughter and son to drive; they were much easier to teach!

A blast from the past was when I had a mother telephone me for her daughter to have lessons. When I first saw the mother, I thought I knew her from somewhere. She also thought she knew me, but neither of us mentioned it. It took a couple of weeks to realise we had worked together ages ago when she was a temporary typist in an office I worked in. Also, our daughters had gone to nursery school together. I taught her daughters to drive, and as her husband was a car mechanic, he started servicing my car.

Another surprise was a telephone call from a school friend wanting me to teach his son and, eventually, his daughter. I felt honoured that he and his wife (we were also at school together) entrusted me to teach their kids. However, it felt a little strange that years later, this was happening, as it did with other friends' offspring.

Personal hygiene can be an issue when you teach people to drive in the confined space of a car. I have taught a few smelly people to drive and have discreetly opened the window to let fresh air into the car. One lad working on a building site on a hot summer day thought he could get in my car without washing off his sweat or changing his clothes. I told him to go back indoors to wash and change. Then I only gave him the remaining time of his lesson. It did not happen again. I remember escaping from someone who asked for lessons. I was in a petrol station shop paying for petrol, and the attendant could see my car through the shop window. They asked if I was the driving instructor and if they could book lessons with me. I could smell their body odour from the opposite side of the counter. I said I was fully booked and quickly excused myself. However, there have been a couple of occasions where a terrible smell had to be dealt with!

The first occasion was with a new pupil, and it was a little embarrassing. I picked her up from home and drove to where I would start teaching new students. After we parked, we both got out of the car to change seats and when we settled down, there was this terrible smell. She was looking at me, and I at her, both of us sniffing the air, wondering what on earth it could be. Then we realised she had trod in the dog's poo. She tried to scrape it off her shoe on the kerb, but I could not clean the rubber mat as it was between the grooves. So, we carried on the lesson with the windows wide open, and after the lesson, I had to go home and deal with the mat, which was not pleasant, I can tell you. When I went to pick up my next pupil, the car still smelt of it, and I had to explain what had happened, spraying air freshener all around. The smell seemed to stay in the car for the entire week, or maybe it had got up my nose.

The second occasion where we dealt with a foul smell was as we followed a tractor pulling a silage trailer. We were in a country lane and got stuck behind it. However, we tried to keep as far back from it as possible but had to follow it for at least a mile before overtaking it. It smelt so bad it hurt our noses, and we could not breathe properly. It was disgusting, and it beat the dog poo.

CHAPTER THREE

UNUSUAL SITUATIONS

AN ANECDOTE FROM A COLLEAGUE'S PUPIL...

Instructor, "Press the clutch down to see how far you have to press it." The pupil took their seat belt off and pressed the clutch with their hand!

A lady whose son, Peter, suffered from a learning disability rang me. She said he wanted to learn to drive and asked if I would take him on. I said I would, but it may be two to three years before he is ready for a driving test. She said that was alright because he wanted to drive and would pay for lessons himself. It took him two and a half years to learn, and he passed his driving test for the first time.

Peter's family was ingenious in teaching him the Highway Code because it was just questions asked at the end of the practical test when he learnt to drive. Implementation of the theory test was not until 1996.

They put pictures and notes on the walls and fridge, making him learn until he could precisely recite the Code.

This paid off so well that when asked the questions on his test, he repeated the answers word for word from the Code. We had a few hiccups while he was learning, a lot of laughing and a lot of resentment by him towards other drivers who did not abide by the rules of the road.

"Why do the other drivers not drive as they should?" he asked with frustration one day as another driver cut him up. "I want to shout and have a go at them."

"Unfortunately, Peter, some do not. They should know the rules of the road, especially those taught by driving instructors. But when they drive by themselves and get more confident, sadly, the rules and regulations get lost in their heads, and they drive without due care and attention. Many drivers, especially old-hand drivers, would not pass their driving test without having refresher lessons with an instructor. Many probably have not read the Highway Code since passing their driving test. Regrettably, because they behave that way, you must have your wits about you to keep clear of them and be safe," I explained. "What do you think could happen if you shouted at them and they were not nice?" I asked.

"Well, I suppose they could get mad at me and even chase or run me off the road," he said worriedly.

"Precisely. So keep calm and carry on, as the saying goes," I said.

He understood our conversation, but sometimes there were a few mumblings under his breath! More explaining about road rage is later in the book.

However, a big issue was his drinking of tea or water before each driving lesson! His mum was trying to get him to take responsibility for himself and not drink too much before his two-hour lesson. Regrettably, he drank too much on two occasions. On the first occasion, we had to make haste to the toilet facilities in the town. His mum always came out when we got back to see how he had got on, and I had to tell her about the problem. She said she would ensure it did not happen again, but unfortunately, it did with more significant consequences. We were out of town, and he said he desperately wanted to go to the loo. I told him to hold it until we returned to town, but the inevitable happened. Yes, he wet the driver's seat! He felt embarrassed, but I was not cross with him. However, I cut the lesson short to get him home for his sake and mine. Him, because of his wet trousers, and mine to clean and dry the seat for my next pupil. His mum saw us return early and ran out of the house to see what had happened. It horrified her when I explained the predicament and apologised while telling him off. She made it abundantly clear it would never happen again, and she would keep a close eye on him in the future. It did not happen again, thankfully!

A lady in her forties wanted to learn to drive to gain independence so she did not have to rely on her ill husband. Unfortunately, her husband was against the idea, but she would not let that stop her. Luckily, she worked, had her own money, and was a fast learner. However, she had a different demeanour when I picked her up for a particular lesson. She was nervous and short-tempered with me, and it was as though she had never driven a car before. Finally, I got her to park up, hoping to calm her down.

"What's up, Sandra?" I asked.

She burst into tears and said, "I bought myself a little mini and went out practising with my husband. He was horrible and told me I was no good or ever would be."

I was furious and said, "He's talking rubbish. Don't drive with him again. We'll show him ."

After a long chat, she decided not to give up and to ignore him. She passed her test the first time and was ecstatic. I asked her how she would break the news to her husband. She said she would post her pass certificate to him rather than tell him, and hopefully, would not be there when the post came and could prepare herself for when she got home. I was dying to know what he had said about her passing, so I rang her to find out. The plan had gone wrong because she was home with him when the letter came. He carried a bundle of books to take into the garage, saw the letter addressed to him, and asked her to open it. Knowing what it was but not looking at it, she held it out for him to read. He read it and was so shocked that he dropped the books he was carrying and had to sit down. I saw her a few months later in the town. She told me everything was fine, and he had been out with her in the car and praised her driving. He also realised it took the pressure off him with her being able to drive.

A similar circumstance happened with a lady in her sixties who I taught. Her husband was also against her learning to drive and gave her no encouragement. Where she lived, the parking spaces provided were on an angle. I taught her to reverse bay park my car in a space between two cars so she would be confident to park their car (which was the same size as mine) after she passed her test. She managed it one day without my instruction, and we knew her husband had been watching her through the kitchen window.

"So, what did your husband say after you had so skilfully parked the car on the last lesson?" I cheerfully asked.

"Well, he wasn't complimentary," she said. "Probably because it took him ages to get to grips with it. He's not good at parking anywhere, anyway. We went to the local supermarket, and because there were only spaces between two cars available, he wouldn't park. So we drove to another supermarket about 5 miles away, which wasn't so busy, so he didn't have to park between cars. He says it's because he's worried about getting his car knocked. I think it's because he can't park the damn thing!

"Oh dear, perhaps I should give him lessons," I laughingly said. "Or you could teach him!"

She chuckled, saying, "I don't think he'll be agreeable." She passed her test on the second attempt and started going to the supermarket alone! Good for her.

A mystery occurred when teaching Bethany to drive. She was getting on OK, and I wanted her to take the theory test so we could think about when to book her practical test. I nagged her about it for quite a while, and finally, she told me she had taken the theory and had passed. Great, she could now book her practical. But time passed, and again, I had to nag her to arrange it. Finally, she told me she had booked it for a particular day and time.

I had given her a lesson the evening before her test and said we would see each other in the morning. When I went to pick her up for the test, her mum was surprised I was there to take Bethany for the practical test because she had not yet passed the theory test! She showed me the letter, giving a future date for the theory test. She was apologetic and could not understand why Bethany had lied. She said she would sort it out and asked if I would continue teaching her when it had blown over. I agreed, and when I saw Bethany, she apologised, and we let bygones be bygones. Eventually, Bethany passed the theory the first time and the practical second time.

In the film Sleepy Hollow, starring Johnny Depp, there was a headless horseman and a tree called 'The Tree of the Dead'. A lad I was teaching to drive lived in a quiet village. His house was on a high bank, so I waited in a lay-by beside a field and a tree which looked like the one in the film. It was alright in the light evenings, but a different story as the nights drew in. Sitting near the tree in the dark, waiting for him, did not appeal to me, and your mind can play tricks on you. I used to turn the radio on loud and have the lights on inside the car. Not that I was worried, you understand! One evening, while waiting, a horse and rider came out from behind the tree and scared the living daylights out of me. Now, what would you do in a situation like that? I was now having a near heart attack and acting like a gibbering idiot as the rider casually trotted off, not realising what was happening to me. When my lad came to the car, he laughed when I told him what had happened. I was glad, however, that the horse rider had a head.

But, unfortunately, the lad was unreliable, often cancelling lessons because of drinking the night before. It was good of him to let me know, but not for me, even though I would charge him for the lesson. Again, he was drinking the night before another lesson with his girlfriend.

She telephoned me at 1 o'clock in the morning to tell me he was too drunk to have his lesson that day. My husband was unimpressed when he answered the telephone and used a few choice words. I then decided enough was enough and did not see the lad again. I was not disappointed.

I taught a girl who followed a subculture but accordingly dressed subtly. However, when I picked her up for a particular lesson, she dressed less subtly because she was going to a nightclub after her lesson. It was a good job that I was a female instructor because I do not think a male could have coped with her outfit.

One day she asked what she should wear for her test as she had heard rumours that examiners judge you on your appearance.

"Examiners are not supposed to," I replied. "However, if you're worried, wear a T-shirt with jeans." Which she did.

Unfortunately, she failed the first test because she emergency stopped for a squirrel, and there was a car behind her, thankfully not too close.

"I don't care about failing. At least the squirrel is still alive," she solemnly said when I spoke to her.

"But, you realise the car behind you could have hit you with you braking so hard," I replied.

"Yes, I know, but I couldn't run over the poor thing," she answered.

"Sometimes, it's them or you," I said. "But I know how you feel."

She passed on the second attempt with no squirrels this time.

A couple of lads I taught named Dan, who I will call Dan 1 and Dan 2, went to a party, and Dan 2 was worse for wear because of drinking too much. Dan 1 had also been drinking, but less than Dan 2; however, Dan 2 wanted to drive home. Dan 1 took his keys away and instead drove home! Regrettably, he got pulled up by the police for not having headlights on and breathalysed. Of course, he was over the limit and banned from driving for a year, with penalty points and a fine. He also thought he would have to retake his driving test.

I was teaching his mum to drive, and she asked if I could give him refresher lessons because he had not driven for two years and prepare him for retaking his driving test. I told her to ensure he had to retake it, as sometimes this is not the case, but she assured me he did because he had said so. So, I began giving him lessons and asked him to show me his licence. Three double lessons went by until he brought out the letter, unopened. When I opened it, it contained his full driving licence, sent to him a year before.

"Dan," I said, looking at him in disbelief. "This is your full driving licence!"

"No, it isn't," he said, looking at me as though I was stupid.

"Oh yes, it is," I said, laughing. "And you have had it the past year sitting in a drawer. Look, it's pink. Your mum's provisional licence is green. You only got penalty points, banned for a year and a fine. You don't have to retake your test."

I cannot tell you the swear words he came out with. Still, I reassured him he hadn't wasted his money because he had 6 hours of refresher lessons and would be alright to go back on the road. He said he thought the licence was provisional and could not afford to have lessons. So he flung the letter into his drawer and did not open it; which is where it stayed for another year. However, he could have been back on the road a year earlier.

When I saw his mum for her lesson, she said, "Don't even ask!"

Another couple of lads I taught had also gone to a party and drank, but they did not take a car. However, after they got home, they were hungry, so they took the car down to the town to get some food. On the way home, one of them threw a drink can out of the window, and the police were behind them, so they got pulled over. So the driver got the same as Dan 1! Stupidity is not a strong enough word!

On another occasion, teaching a lad to drive took a long time as he worked away from home, but he was finally ready to take his test and passed. Working away again, he and his boss drank in the pub near their lodgings. They could not park their van outside where they were staying when first arriving, so they parked outside the pub. When they came out, his boss told him to move the van to where the lodgings were as there was now a space. But the police were in a police car near the pub, saw him enter the van, and breathalysed him immediately. Regretfully, he was over the prescribed limit for alcohol and charged him with 'being in charge of a vehicle with intent to drive'. He got banned from driving after only having his licence for a month!

FACT – The alcohol limits are as follows:

In England, Wales, and Northern Ireland, the alcohol limit for drivers is 80 milligrams of alcohol per 100 millilitres of blood. 35 micrograms per 100 millilitres of breath. 107 milligrams per 100 millilitres of urine. In Europe, the limit is mostly less, usually 50 milligrams per 100 millilitres of blood. In Scotland, the alcohol limit for drivers differs from the rest of the UK. The limit is 50 milligrams of alcohol per 100 millilitres of blood. 22 micrograms of alcohol per 100 millilitres of breath. 67 milligrams per 100 millilitres of urine. (At the time of writing.)

So the moral of the above stories is DON'T DRINK AND DRIVE.

Sometimes cancellation of tests happens because of unforeseen circumstances, and mostly you get a notification in good time. However, if an examiner is ill on the day, and there is no time to let the candidate know, you could arrive at the test centre and find they have cancelled your test. This happened to the mum of Dan 1, who thought he had to retake his test. An examiner came into the waiting room and called her name, but it was to tell her that the test would not go ahead. She broke down and cried because she had been so uptight about taking the test, and it was such an anticlimax. However, it was a blessing in disguise because she was not so uptight the next time and passed on her first attempt. Still, that is nothing compared to what happened in the following story.

When one of my girls was nearly ready for her test, I told her to book it, and we aimed to prepare her for that day. However, her name was not called when we got to the test centre. I wondered what would happen, as too many candidates were in the waiting room. So, before taking his candidate for their test, an examiner telephoned the booking office to find out the problem. They informed him her sister had telephoned the booking office and cancelled the test, saying she was ill. They were not getting on, and we were both shocked to think her sister could stoop so low as to cancel her driving test. I drove her home because she was so distressed.

Crying her eyes out, she said, "I can't believe my sister would do this to me. She must hate me. I know we haven't been getting on well lately. How could she do such a thing?"

"I don't think she would go that far to get back at you," I said. "It could be the booking office making a terrible mistake by cancelling the wrong candidate," I said, trying to reassure her.

When we returned to her house, she telephoned the booking office to ask if the information was correct. Indeed, they said her sister had telephoned a week ago, cancelling the test. She contacted her dad at work, but I had to speak to him as she was so upset. He then talked to her and said to say nothing to her sister when she got home, and he and her mum would sort it out that evening. Her sister denied cancelling the test, which caused such disquiet in the household because they did not know whether to believe her. Her dad also telephoned the booking office and got the same story. We could only assume if her sister told the truth, the booking office had made a terrible mistake. If it was them cancelling the wrong candidate, they also caused a lot of unnecessary unease in the house. She booked another test but kept it secret, and she passed. About a year later, I started teaching her sister. She first told me she had not cancelled the test and was so sorry about what had happened; we did not mention it again. She also passed her test for the first time. So, *WHODUNNIT?* I lay my bets on the booking office.

I taught another two sisters to drive. The eldest was a good girl, always there and on time for her lessons and passing the theory and practical tests for the first time. No trouble with her. Sadly, her sister was a different kettle of fish. Late for lessons, not at home, getting her out of bed, etc. Then a time came when I had to reprimand her when I saw her driving her parent's car while they and her sister were away on holiday. Parked up on the left with a pupil, to my alarm, I saw her driving past me with five other people in her parent's car. I had to take a double look because I could not believe my eyes. When I next saw her, I said,

"Do you know, I was sitting at the side of the road with another pupil the other day, and I saw your twin sister driving your parent's car."

"I haven't got a twin sister," she coyly answered.

"Really," I replied. "Well, you must have a doppelgänger because I saw the double of you driving a car of the same make and model your parents have!"

She then had a worried look on her face. "Please don't tell my parents," she pleaded. "I promise I won't do it again."

I scolded her, saying, "That was a stupid thing to do. You could have had a serious accident, putting yourself and your friends at risk by showing off. So, why on earth did you do it?" She did not have an answer.

I went to pick her up for her next lesson just after her parents returned from holiday, and her mum answered the front door.

"Sorry, Brenda," she said. "She's not in. That girl, I don't know what to do with her. Do you know, whilst we were away, she had a party? So, I've got drink stains and broken glass on my carpets, and somehow, the bath got burnt!"

I did not squeal on her, holding my tongue, but thought, "That's not the only thing that happened." She eventually passed the theory and practical tests the first time, and I hope she behaves herself while on the road.

Abbey had a lesson on her lunch break and wanted to practice the left reverse corner. We were on a no-through road, but there was a left turning just before the end. So we parked up to begin the manoeuvre, noticing a car parked about 15ft away from us with the vehicle's windows steamed up. Also, the car was slightly rocking, so we sat there waiting to see what was happening. Then two heads popped up and down again.

"Oh, what do you think is going on there?" Abbey asked with a grin.

"Your guess is as good as mine. Probably it's a clandestine affair during the lunch break," I smirked.

We were cracking up laughing and carried on with the manoeuvre, practising it several times, just to be awkward. We drove off about fifteen minutes later. Hopefully, they were still in time to get back to work!

While practising the reverse corner at another junction with Christine, a drunk man came along and peed up the wall near the corner. Perhaps Christine was not manoeuvring the car adequately to his liking and thought he would give his opinion by relieving himself.

"Charming," said Christine. "I don't think that's very nice of him."

"Well, he is quite drunk. So let us carry on as though he's not there," I replied. "As long as he doesn't pee up my car," I laughed.

Speaking of peeing and drunk situations, we have had a drunk man run out into the middle of the road we were driving along and put his hand up to stop us. My pupil had to emergency stop to avoid running him over. He started banging on the car's bonnet, shouting abuse at us, but then staggered off to annoy somebody else. It startled my pupil, but he handled the situation just so.

On entering the High Street where I used to teach, we approached a mini-roundabout where four drunken people were crossing the road. My pupil was stopping the car to let them finish crossing, when the last man thought it funny to fall down, making out she had hit him. Not funny!

Boy, was I mad and got out of the car yelling, "What the hell do you think you're doing? Idiot. You've just frightened the life out of my pupil because of your stupidity."

His friends laughed, saying, "He's only mucking about."

"Well, you're all a bunch of idiots if you think it's funny," I retorted. "You don't muck about like that in front of any vehicle, let alone a learner's car. You could have put her off learning to drive for life."

The people in the pub across the road saw what had happened and were also laughing, which did not help. Poor Margaret was shaking, and I had to calm her down. I read somewhere that a joke can fail in one of two ways. It can be too benign and, therefore, boring, or it can be too much of a violation and, therefore, offensive. This was definitely the latter.

As a driving instructor, you need an extremely strong bladder and know where all the toilet facilities are. So I would time my pupils' lessons so I could pop home or use a loo in town before my next lesson. One day, I hoped to get home at around 11 am as usual, but regrettably, my pupil Natalie hit a wheel against the kerb. I checked the wheel, and it seemed alright, so we carried on, but while we were on a small dual carriageway, the tyre went down. We pulled into a lay-by to get it sorted. Now I know how to change a wheel, but the locking nut on the wheel is tough to loosen. I would generally ring my husband to help us. I call him my fourth emergency service, after police, fire and ambulance services! However, he was not well that day, so rather than disturb him, I rang the RAC, but there was at least a two-hour wait. We waited to see if they would turn up earlier, but then Natalie suggested telephoning her husband to see if he could come and help. It was nearing 11 am, and my bladder told me I needed the loo. Oh dear, the nearest loo was at least three miles away, and while we were waiting for her husband, who kindly said he would come out to us, my bladder was getting fuller and fuller. We laughed, but I would burst if I did not go. So we decided the best thing was to open the front and rear nearside passenger doors, with me between the two, so I could go.

"We're not teacher or pupil now; we're friends," Natalie said, laughing her head off.

"Oh dear, this is not good. There's steam coming up!" I shrieked. "Goodness knows what the passing drivers are thinking. I hope nobody stops."

Thankfully, they did not and oh, what a relief! Her husband eventually turned up and changed the wheel for me, but for the future, I need to go to the gym to build up muscles in my arms to undo that locking nut!

While negotiating a roundabout to take the right exit. My pupil signalled, checked both mirrors and her left shoulder, and started positioning to exit the roundabout because it was clear. Suddenly a car came hurtling past us on our left, cutting us up to take the exit we wanted (hence the importance of checking both mirrors and shoulder glance). The car shot off as though nothing had happened. We were on our way to the test car park, and a man approached us after we parked.

"OK, we're in for a moan," I said to my pupil and cracked open my window.

"I am so sorry for cutting you up on the roundabout back there," he apologetically said. "I don't know why I did it. Remembering my driving lessons, it happened to me. I know how learning to drive feels. I'm so very sorry."

I was aghast; someone was actually apologising for what they had done! Am I dreaming? Pinch me to wake me up. All I could give him was a thank you, staring at him as though he were a figment of my imagination.

After he walked away, I asked my pupil, "Well, what do you make of that then?" We were dumbfounded!

When I started teaching, I had a call from a man who lived in an area well known for being rough. Sadly, decent people living on the estate got tarred with the same brush.

Many of them were re-housed there by the local council because of circumstances beyond their control. I did not tell him I was the instructor, so he did not know the instructor was a woman. Also, because he lived in a block of flats, I asked him to meet the instructor on the pavement. I talked it over with my husband as I was a little dubious about taking him on, so we settled on the idea I would drive past if I did not like the look of him. Well, he looked alright to me, and he was. He passed his test the first time, and from him, I gained practically all of his family, ranging from his brothers, sisters, aunts, uncles, nieces and nephews. Think about how much business I would have lost without teaching him. Even moving to a different location and not taking on new pupils from my previous area, I had a member of his family begging me to teach them. But I could not as it was too far away.

I taught Sylvia, an astrologer and medium, who predicted the future. I had a girl who had a bad run on her driving test, failed and was distraught about it. She was a friend of Sylvia's daughter, but Sylvia did not know her daughter's friend was taking her test. However, when she got in the car and started driving, she was not her usual confident self.

"Are you alright, Sylvia?" I asked.

"Something isn't right," she said. "I can feel tension through the steering wheel."

"What's happened?" she asked. "It's upsetting me."

We drove a little further, and then she said she needed to stop because it was too much. I told her about her daughter's friend taking her test and how bad it was, and that was it. Sylvia could feel the tension of the girl through the steering wheel. Strange indeed. We finished the lesson because she could not concentrate.

Creepy!

A driving instructor in our local area was known for touching the girls, and I had quite a few of them come to me for lessons. They would tell me how he would help them put their seat belt on, or he needed to hold their leg to feel the tension when they used the clutch, or he would put his hand on theirs when they changed the gear. His reputation grew, so he changed the name of his driving school. Eventually, people got wise, and his business started going downhill. Finally, the father of a girl went to his house to confront him and reported him to the DVSA. In due course, he had to cease trading.

There was another instructor whose actions were like the one above. He dressed inappropriately, especially in the summer. I talked to him about where his hand was when walking with a young girl to the test centre office. He tried to justify himself by saying she was a relation of his. Really! Did that give him the excuse? Gradually his reputation got the better of him.

FACT – If any abuse happens to you, report it to GOV.UK-Complain about a Driving Instructor, and they will deal with the culprit.

Another instructor, we all thought, had lost his mind because he bought a 4 x 4 and renamed his driving school. I will not say the name, but it was derogatory. On the tailgate where the spare wheel was, he also had a picture of the name on its cover. This appealed to some people, but others disapproved. The examiners refused to go out on tests with the cover on the spare wheel. The police also pulled him over and told him to remove it as it was offensive. Eventually, he reverted to his old school name.

CHAPTER FOUR

OTHER DRIVERS

AN ANECDOTE FROM A COLLEAGUE'S PUPIL…

A polite doctor, referring to an Audi driver behind, said, "I'm going to lend you my endoscope if you get any closer."

I want to thank all considerate drivers who are patient and understanding of learners. After all, we were all learners once upon a time. However, instructors and learners can suffer abuse almost daily. The abusers like to let you know learners are a nuisance or a pain in the butt and have no right to be on the road. Hence, the 'L' plate is like a red rag to a bull. One of my colleagues had a brilliant way of getting rid of arrogant drivers at junctions. He would get out of his car with a duster, dust the 'L' plate, go to the car behind and say, "Can you see the 'L' plate better, mate?" That usually defused the situation.

I picked Anna up for her first driving lesson at 7 pm, and it was just getting dark. I chose a long, straight, quiet road and parked in a lay-by. So, after explaining some theory to her, we pulled out of the lay-by. We took it easy but not unduly slow when a car came behind us. As there was no oncoming traffic, he could easily have overtaken us. But no! He stayed behind us, hooting the horn and flashing the headlights. This was putting her off, so we pulled into the next lay-by to get rid of him. However, he pulled in behind us. He got out of his car and approached us, so I quickly locked the doors. He banged on the driver's window, and I told Anna to open the window slightly, but he put his fingers between the window and the car's body.

He started yelling at me, "What do you think you are doing bringing this girl out at this time of night? You have no right to be on the road. I am going to report you to the police."

"Could you please go away? You are distressing my pupil," I answered, trying to keep myself composed. "Mind your own business."

He was highly aggressive, even though he had a woman and child in his car.

"Anna," I said. "Gently close the window, but remember, his fingers are there." He quickly removed his fingers as the window began closing.

However, he again banged on the window, but we ignored him, and finally, he returned to his car.

"I'm so sorry, Anna, you experienced this aggression in your first lesson. You must take no notice of him and remember you have every right to be on the road, even at this time of night," I reassured her.

"Do you still want to carry on with the lesson?"

"Yes, yes, I'm OK. The man shook me up, but I want to carry on," she courageously said.

After her lesson, I spoke to her mum and dad about the situation, worried she might become anxious about what happened as the week went by and give up learning. However, they were understanding, and she continued lessons. Luckily nothing else happened, and confidently she passed the first time.

Another pupil, Alison, was waiting to get onto a dual carriageway from a side road. It was hectic, and we could not get out. Then, after a few moments, a man came behind us and decided we had taken too long to move. So he started hooting at us, not just a beep but a continuous hoot. Alison was getting so worried and nervous that I feared she would pull out into the traffic. So, I kept my foot over my footbrake, just in case she did. I soooo wanted to get out of my car, get his keys, and throw them into the bushes. But, finally, there was a space, and we started moving out into the left-hand lane, and he charged into the right-hand lane to overtake us.

"Don't look at him," I said. "Don't give him the satisfaction of scaring you."

"But he has scared me," Alison fearfully said. "I don't want to do this any longer. I want to go home now."

Sadly, when we got home, she ran indoors, crying uncontrollably, saying she did not want to drive again. I spoke to her mum, explaining what had happened. Sadly, the trauma was too much for her, and she gave up on learning. However, I hope she took up the gauntlet later in life and learnt to drive.

Another dual-carriageway incident occurred while we sat on the central reservation, waiting to cross to the opposite side. It was teeming with vehicles from our left travelling up to 70 mph. Suddenly, there was a banging on the driver's window. A woman in the car behind us thought we were taking too long to cross the carriageway.

"Why haven't you gone yet?" she yelled. "You could've gone by now!"

"Excuse me!" I answered. "What makes you think we could've gone by now?"

"You've been sitting here for ages," she yelled back.

"And we'll be sitting here for ages more if you don't clear off," I quipped.

"Could I have been gone by now?" my pupil asked.

"Not if you value your life," I answered.

The woman returned to her car in a huff. We then could go leaving her in the dust.

While waiting at a busy junction in a lesson with Gemma, a car about six-car lengths behind us started hooting. Looking in her side mirror, she could see the car, and it was her sister hooting. After we concentrated on getting out of the junction, she told me when her sister started learning to drive, she gave it up. The reason was that people were impatient and hooting her. Finally, after a couple of years, she decided to re-learn and pass her test.

"Now she has the cheek to hoot learner drivers," she said. "Little does she know it's *me* she's hooting! Wait until I see her. I'll give her something to hoot at. I'm going to give her a right old rollicking."

"Good for you, Gemma," I laughingly said. "You give her what for."

"Too right," she replied.

Gemma was obsessed with her lucky red boots, wearing them for all her lessons. She wore them through all the seasons, whatever the weather, and for her test. They had holes in the soles, and her feet got wet when it rained. She wore nothing else because they were comfortable, and she thought it would affect her driving if she wore other footwear. Maybe Gemma was right because she passed the first time. I had another pupil who wore her lucky red shoes and also passed the first time. There must be something about red-foot attire!

My car displayed my driving school name, telephone number and 'L' plates. Driving along a narrow winding country lane (with no passing places), we went about 20/30 mph, sometimes less because the bends were so sharp. There was a 4 x 4 close behind us, carrying two women. When I got home in the evening, my husband asked if I had been teaching along a country lane that afternoon. He told me he had a telephone call from a woman passenger in the 4 x 4 behind me.

She said to him, "I'm 'phoning to complain about one of your driving instructors driving in front of us far too slow."

"What do you want me to do about it?" he asked.

"Well, tell her!" she replied.

"How can I do that? I can't get in touch with her now. She's not allowed to answer her mobile while working or driving. Where are you, and what's the road layout?" he briskly asked.

"We are driving along a narrow country lane. She won't let us pass," she replied.

"Do you know the speed limit, and are there any passing places? Are you the driver?" my husband asked. "If so, you shouldn't be 'phoning me whilst driving."

"No, I'm the passenger," she replied, and then he heard her say to the driver that he was getting 'shirty' and wanted to know the speed limit and whether there were any passing places. A passing place is on a two-way single-track road with only room for one vehicle. So you wait in one on your left or the opposite one for the oncoming vehicle to use. Do the same procedure if a car wants to overtake you.

"I don't know the speed limit," the driver said. "And what's a passing place?"

"Well, it's not good enough that a fully qualified driver doesn't know the speed limit of the road or what a passing place is. The default limit is 60 mph, but if you are driving along a narrow country lane, as you say, keep your speed down. It's not safe to drive fast and be patient, especially as it's a learner driver in front of you," he retorted and put the 'phone down.

I told him I remembered a 4 x 4 behind us getting too close. Also, as we reached the end of the road, turning left, we could see a lorry coming towards us, so we waited because we knew there would not be room for both of us. However, the impatient 4 x 4 driver went around us, straight into the face of the oncoming lorry. So you can imagine the uproar between them and the lorry driver. We, of course, were enjoying the ensuing argument.

When we were at a busy mini-roundabout, one of my girls kept stalling the car because the motorist behind us kept hooting. When I looked around, the driver hand-gestured me. It was early morning with heavy oncoming traffic; therefore, he could not overtake us. So, we got our own back by driving extremely slow until we reached the end of the road, going over two bridges and tackling another mini-roundabout. Perhaps the driver may think again and be more patient in the future.

On another occasion, I gave the motorist behind us time to worry as they were hooting us at a different mini-roundabout where it was too busy to go. While my pupil was driving, I got my notepad, held it up high to ensure the driver could see it, and wrote down their car's registration number. They followed us as we entered another town with a police station. I told my pupil to pull into the police station's car park. That gave them something to think about during the day, wondering if the police would knock on their door for road rage.

As mentioned in the *'Near and Actual Accidents'* chapter, I respect the road and traffic police, who do a great job keeping our roads safe and have been there at the right time. But, sometimes, they take the biscuit. For example, while driving in town and waiting at a busy junction to join a one-way system, the driver behind us had other ideas and started beeping and flashing the headlights. As we entered the one-way system into the right-hand lane, he came alongside us in the left-hand lane, and I am afraid I hand-gestured to him! He then rolled down the driver's window, stuck a card out saying he was the police, and told us to pull over (he was in an unmarked vehicle and on his own). We pulled over about three car lengths away from him. He got out of his car and stood behind it.

"What are you going to do?" Fay asked.

"Well, I'd better see what he's got to say," I said.

So, I did what you should *NOT* do. I got out of the car and walked towards him, keeping my distance. I was told off for it later by Fay's sister, a police officer. He shouted at me, and I interrupted him, but he wanted the first word.

"That's a fine way to teach your pupils how to drive," he yelled and lectured me on how I should behave.

After he ranted and raved, I said, "Now, tell me why you were continually hooting us and flashing your headlights."

"To let you know I was there," was his reply.

I was temporarily speechless but then looked at him and said, "What! That's the most unbelievable and ridiculous answer you could give me. But, of course, I knew you were there. You may likely have put my pupil off learning to drive because drivers like you are too impatient. You could see it was busy, and there was no way we could move out."

He answered, "Perhaps we've both learnt a lesson today!"

What a cheek! I had enough by then and went back to my car. Fay's sister said he had no right to pull me over as he was not in uniform, nor should I have got out of the car.

FACT – An unmarked police car can stop vehicles. Still, to comply with the law's provisions, a constable in uniform must be present in the police car. Therefore, if an unmarked car flashes for you to pull over and stop, only stop if you are sure it is the police.

So in retrospect, first, I should not have hand-gestured to him (though he really annoyed me). Second, I should have stayed inside the car or not even stopped, and third, I should have asked to see his ID again. Was he really a police officer? Or I could have driven to the nearest police station. However, you only sometimes think clearly in these situations, which is how you get caught.

Within a short time, I had another incident with the police in the same town. This time we were in a different one-way system with a large central reservation, signalling to turn right in the correct lane, ready to go to the opposite side of the reservation. As we approached the junction, a marked police car came past us on the left-hand side, again hooting the horn at us aggressively. My pupil was so shocked that she panicked and put her foot down on the accelerator, landing us on the grass verge, nearly hitting a tree. Thank goodness for dual controls!

When I got home, I was enraged. So, I rang the police and asked to speak to the officer in charge of the police vehicles. I wanted to make an informal complaint about what had happened. The person I talked to was rude and unhelpful and would not give me his name. My husband tried to speak to him, but the person threatened to put the telephone down if my husband did not let him talk to me again. He still would not put me through, and I informed him I would take the matter further in writing. Within an hour of the telephone call, a police officer rang, saying he was in charge of the police vehicles and asking what the problem was. I related to him about the way the other person spoke to me while trying to make an informal complaint and then explained the incident. He apologised extensively about the situation and said he would bring the complaint about the police officers up at their next meeting. He asked if I had got the registration number of the car involved. Of course, I did not have it, as I was too busy with my pupil, but I told him the time and area where it happened. He said it would be difficult to bring to book the police officers involved as I did not have the number. However, I replied if he mentioned the date, time and place, the officers implicated would know who they were and perhaps think again before acting the same way. I also told him about the first occurrence on the other one-way system. He assured me that in their training, police drivers are advised on how to treat learner drivers. However, he said he would speak to his police drivers and reinstate the directive.

Another occasion involving the police was when in another area, we drove past a police car while they were sitting in a lay-by. The next thing, they were behind us and signalled for us to pull over, which we did. I do not know if, as sometimes suggested, they were trying to get their numbers up for pulling vehicles over for that day, but it certainly felt like it this time.

A young police officer approached me and said, "The 'L' plates are too high on the bonnet. You can't see them in the rear-view mirror."

I replied, "I can't lower them any further because they will blow off the bonnet and have been in that position for the last twenty-odd years. The examiners have never objected to their position, and I can assure you they would complain if they were too high."

"You can tie them onto the bumper," he said.

"Go look at the bumper and tell me how I can do it," I suggested.

He came back after looking and said, "The law states." But before he could continue, I said, "I know what the law states, but I am not moving them." He then walked off!

It infuriated me to be pulled over for no good reason and upset my pupil. It then dawned on me a little while later how he knew you could not see the 'L' plates in the rear-view mirror, as he was not in front of me. I heard nothing more from the police and did not alter the position of the 'L' plates because I checked drivers in front of me could see them in their rear-view mirror. I am sure this was a wind-up.

I had a police car following us around the route we were taking on a lesson. I wondered why he was doing this. It made my lad nervous, and I had to reassure him he was not doing anything wrong. I told him that maybe a brake light was not working. The trouble is that you can check that all lights are working before you leave your house, but they can fail as you drive. Some vehicles have warning signs, but mine did not. So we continued with the lesson, and the police car followed us to my lad's house, which was on an unmade road, and pulled up beside us.

I opened my window and said, "Can I help you, officer?"

I got a curt reply. "Brake light, mend it!" Then he drove off.

The police officer I spoke to (as mentioned above) in charge of police vehicles told me they trained police drivers to be aware of learner drivers. Subsequently, it has not come down the line at all well, or I have been unfortunate with unsympathetic officers. However, something nice happened whilst on a lesson with my daughter. It started snowing and came down heavily, so we pulled into a lay-by. A police car pulled up, and the officer came to ensure we were alright.

A personal incident happened many years ago when driving around 10 o'clock at night. Shame the police were not about when this happened. I was on a dual carriageway system and driving 70 mph when a car overtook me, came in front of me, and slowed right down; it was a male driver, so I stayed behind him for a while. I then overtook him and returned to the left lane further up the road. This happened a few more times. Finally, we were in town, and I was in front of him driving through the high street, but I knew there was a right turn ahead. I did not slow down or signal and shot off to the right, and he missed the turning. I quickly got home and opened the garage doors and the car into the garage. As I was doing this, I could hear his car racing around the roads, and as I peered over the fence, I saw him drive past my house. It shook me up, but pleased I kept my nerve and lost him. I admit I was nervous about seeing him again on the same route I frequently had to take, but thankfully never did.

Just to add. How alarmed would you be if you had a vehicle coming towards you in a one-way system, then the driver dared to motion you to reverse so they could get through! Obviously, you take no notice and sit there until *they* reverse. Even more alarming is to have vehicles on roundabouts taking the wrong direction and approaching you head-on. Then, for good measure, drivers who find themselves on the opposite side of a dual carriageway travelling into the face of oncoming traffic. Yes, this happens. Seen and involved in these terrifying situations.

CHAPTER FIVE

YOU CAN'T PLEASE PEOPLE ALL OF THE TIME

AN ANECDOTE FROM A COLLEAGUE'S PUPIL…

Talking about birthdays, a pupil said, "My birthday present was awful. I had a driving lesson with you!"

In the years I have been an instructor, I have had hundreds of pupils kindly give me great reviews or recommend me. However, I had two pupils who did not. The first one was at least two to three years after I had taught her to drive. She had failed her test on observation. I accompanied her on the driving test and saw where she had not correctly judged to the right. She pulled out of the junction, causing another vehicle to slow down. She was upset and thought she had enough time to go before the car reached her, but she accepted the examiner's decision. She was off to university, so we discussed she would find an instructor where she was studying to retake the test in that area. I spoke to her mother and reiterated the conversation, and she agreed. It ended amicably, or so I thought. A few years later, I moved away from the area where I was teaching and, being well-known, did not have to advertise for pupils. Going to a new place where people did not know me, I had to promote myself, so I joined Facebook. I found a page with reviews for the instructors in my old area, and to my amazement, one from this girl who gave me a critical review and put her name on it. It devastated me.

I looked up my old records and took the chance to ring the telephone number I had. Her brother answered and told me she was on holiday with their parents and he could take a message. I said he would not like what I had to say and related the review to him. He was shocked and said he would get it sorted. I told him I would take further action if it was not off the site before the end of the week. I would have liked to have been a fly on the wall when she returned from the holiday. She removed the review immediately.

The second review was a cowardly, anonymous review. After a few investigations, I had a good idea who it was. It was a nasty review, but I could not have it removed because 'Google My Business' refused to do so. I could only counteract it by asking some of my previous pupils to put good reviews on the site to make hers look foolish, and they did. I was so grateful to them for helping me. On the plus side, I still receive Christmas cards from pupils I taught years ago. They address the envelope 'To the Best Driving Instructor in the Whole Wide World'. Nice to know I pleased some people! Thank you.

But sometimes, in this job, you think you are being taken for a ride (like the pun?). I had been nagging two girls I taught to drive to book the theory test as they were getting near the practical test standard. However, unbeknown to me, they had taken the theory test and passed the practical test in their own cars. They then booked me out! How rude!

Also, it can be very annoying when an instructor sees a pupil shopping or elsewhere when they have cancelled their lesson for that day because they are ill or some other excuse. I remember a pupil who told me she had to look after her grandmother for the day, as she was sick. Unfortunately, I saw her walking along the road with her boyfriend, nowhere near her grandmother's house! She was embarrassed, apologetic and out of pocket when I confronted her in the next lesson and charged her.

When you work with somebody close, you must be able to gel with them, but sometimes I would take on a person and get bad vibes. Since I knew how I felt, I ensured it did not affect how I treated them. But sometimes it was tough having to be careful about what I said and knowing I could not joke. I had a man book a course of lessons, but I had a bad feeling about him. He was surly, and he would argue about how I was teaching him (why did he need me then?), and I found it quite difficult to keep my temper. One day he got into the car, and before we had reached the end of his road, he had already started being rude.

"OK, stop the car. I've had enough of you!" I angrily said.

"What's the matter with you? You're a bit moody," he retorted.

"What! You have such a cocky attitude and are rude to me. I'm not putting up with it any longer. Get out of my car," I retaliated.

"Oh, I am so sorry, Brenda. I apologise, and I will behave myself," he sheepishly said. "Please, will you carry on teaching me to drive?"

Like an idiot, I agreed but said if he was rude in the future, that would be it. The lessons continued, and now and again, his rudeness would try to break through, but I stopped it in its tracks.

In one lesson, we were recapping the controlled stop (emergency stop). We had practised this before, but Dean needed to improve it. So I gave him another explanation, and we set off. He still had trouble, and I saw he was getting frustrated, so I got him to park on the left to talk to him about it. As he was still finding it difficult, we agreed to continue the lesson by practising other points and return to the emergency stop another day. As he drove, I asked him to take a right corner. He looked at me with a distorted expression and talked to me like a slowed-down record. I had to take over the steering wheel and use my dual controls to stop us from crashing. I got parked up, but he had passed out by this time. He had had an epileptic fit! I did not know what to do and was shouting at him, hoping he would come round, which, after a few moments, he did, but dazed. Somehow, I got him to change seats so I could drive him home. He was more lucid when we got home and admitted he had epilepsy.

When he began his lessons, I checked his driving licence and noted it was a restricted three-year licence, which means there was a health problem. Still, being naïve in my career, I had not asked him about the issue. I told him I would report him to the DVLA and get his licence revoked, and he pleaded with me not to, but I went straight home to ring the DVLA. However, when I arrived home, my husband said he had an angry father on the telephone, saying I had no right to report his son to the DVLA. I rang the father, but before I could explain what had happened, he started shouting at me, saying,

"You have no right to report him to the DVLA. There's nothing wrong with him. It was probably the DRINK he had the night before when he played Bingo. That's what probably affected his drugs and set off the fit!"

"Are you telling me he was drinking last night? That's even worse. No drink should touch his lips if he has a lesson the next day. Where is the responsibility he and you should have? I am reporting him, and he will have to face the consequences," I hit back and put the telephone down.

I could not believe what he was telling me. If you know you will drive the next day, even in ordinary circumstances, you should not drink the evening before. You could still be over the limit. He said when they went to Bingo sessions, his son could still hear the numbers being called even if he was not totally with it and be able to tick them off the sheet when he came around. He also had a driving job lined up for when he passed his test. I was in utter disbelief and said going to Bingo and driving were two entirely different things, and he should not be on the road.

After the conversation, I rang the DVLA to report him. If you have a seizure, you must immediately report it to the authorities and stop driving. After what his father told me, it seemed there was no intention of doing so, and he did not seem to care about his son's life or that of others. If you have epilepsy or diabetes, you must be sensible and abide by the strict rules. See GOV.UK Epilepsy and Driving and GOV.UK Diabetes and Driving.

Another lad I taught was also quite rude, and I needed the patience of a saint when on a lesson with him. He thought he knew everything and was cocksure of himself. I was also teaching his girlfriend to drive and had taught her sister. The only reason I kept him on was because of them. I do not know how they put up with him. Also, I taught a woman to drive who worked with him and said nobody in the office liked him because of his rudeness. I dreaded his lessons. After a while, I thought about how to stop teaching him. Then, he gave me the opportunity when he had his licence stolen.

"OK, you had better apply for a duplicate, and you'll have to pay for it," I said.

"I'm not paying for another licence; it's not my fault," he said, looking at me as though I had said something horrifying.

"Well, the DVLA won't issue you another one if you don't pay for it," I explained.

He had a few rows with the DVLA over his refusal to pay for a duplicate. So he could not take the driving test without his licence in his pocket, and he was cutting his nose off to spite his face. Now I also had an excellent excuse to get rid of him. Hooray!

As I explained things to him, another cocky lad in his first lesson told me he already knew everything and could drive anyway.

He said, "I already know how to drive; I don't need help. This is my mum's idea. 'You've got to have some lessons to pass your test,' she says. I don't think I need them, but she's paying, not me. After all, my mate passed the first time, and he's as thick as a brick. So did my sister, and she's not that good. How hard can it be?"

I became intrigued by what he said, so I told him to show me if he knew it all. He started the engine and stalled it about five times when trying to move off. I had to talk him through the moving away procedure, but then I kept quiet. As he drove, he crunched the gear into second, started speeding up, not changing gear, and then somehow started to kangaroo along the road. By this time, I had enough, so I told him to pull over into a lay-by, though I had to do the braking. He was red-faced, agreed he did not know it all, and apologised. After which, we got on fine with each other, with him passing for the first time.

I started teaching a girl, Laura, who had been having lessons with another instructor but could not get on with him. She was lovely but quick to show annoyance if she had a problem with something. I got her to test standard, and she booked her test. Knowing how her temper would flare if she did something wrong, I was worried about what she would do if it happened on the test, so I asked if I could go out with her, to which she had no objection.

On her first test, she drove out of the car park but took a left turn too fast. A parked car was just around the corner, and the examiner had to brake and push the steering wheel out to avoid it. I was waiting for her to say something, but she kept quiet. Then, she stopped checking her right shoulder on the second test before moving off. I was telepathically trying to get her to do it, but no. So another failure. However, she was alright with it, and like on the first occasion, she booked her next test via her mobile on the way home. So the third test came, and she was doing well until she reached the end of a road to turn right. A vehicle was approaching from her left, signalling to turn right and slowing down to take the corner. Unfortunately, she went to pull out of the junction before the vehicle had completed the manoeuvre, and the examiner braked. That was it! She flew into a raging temper, swearing at the examiner, telling him she wasn't driving any longer and using other profanities. He wanted her to carry on driving so he could get her to park in a safe place, but unfortunately, she was still ranting and raving. So I leaned forward and asked him if he wanted me to drive back to the test centre as the DVSA forbade examiners to drive the car; he was happy with my suggestion. When we got there, I apologised to him, on her behalf, for the unacceptable behaviour, and on the way home, I gave her a stern talking-to. When we arrived, she got out of the car, slammed the door and did not apologise to me.

About three months after her test, I rang her. We got on with each other by ignoring her tantrums, and I can give people the benefit of the doubt. Her mum answered the telephone and said she was asleep, but she would wake her.

"No, no, don't wake her," I pleaded.

"It's OK," her mum said. "She'll be alright."

She woke her, and I heard her saying, "Laura, it's Brenda on the 'phone wanting to know what you're doing about your next test."

"I don't want to speak to her!" she irritably answered.

Her mum asked her again. Still, in a gruff voice, she said, "I told you I don't want to speak to her."

She came back on the telephone apologising, and I thought that was it. However, to my amazement, Laura telephoned a couple of weeks later to say she had booked another test. Luckily, I had the space available. When I saw her, she apologised for how she acted and passed her test on the fourth attempt.

Some pupils get upset because they cannot carry out a manoeuvre. Their coordination will not let them achieve what others can, and they need to understand why they cannot do it. One girl, whose mum I had taught to drive, got into a terrible temper. She stopped the car, got out and slammed the door, shouting,

"I never want to get back in the car ever again," and started walking up the road.

I followed her (we were on a quiet side road) and persuaded her to continue with the lesson. She got back in the car but started crying. After we had a long chat, she calmed down. She then passed her test for the first time. So the motto is - 'If at first, you don't succeed, try, try to try again'.

When driving to your driving test, nerves can overcome you, and you may find you need the loo. However, there were no toilets at a couple of test centres I used, and I would ask my pupils if they needed the loo to give time before the test to use those in the High Street. At one of these test centres, we could use the facilities. But, because a candidate got upset about failing the test, they vented their anger by writing, in red, across the wall. '…….. is a pig'. The other office workers in the building and the examiners were a little upset about it, so they banned us all; candidates and instructors.

I have heard stories from some of my pupils about how their friends' instructors have acted. Instructors need a lot of patience with all pupils and even more so when teaching somebody who finds it challenging. Still, as a professional, you must contain yourself and keep calm because most pupils eventually get it. I was told about an instructor who got so angry with a friend of my pupil that he told her to pull over on the left, promptly got out of the car and started banging his fists on the bonnet. It scared her, but luckily it was near the end of her lesson, so they were going home. She booked another lesson with him because she did not want a row, then told her mum and dad, who dealt with the situation.

Another pupil's friend was driving along the road when a van driver stepped partially out in front of them to get into his van but quickly stepped back. The instructor immediately used the dual controls and braked. He angrily got out of the car, held the van driver by his throat, and had him up against his van, swearing at him. He then got back into the car and told her to drive on. However, she refused to carry on and got out of the car to walk home. Good for her.

We were in a queue of traffic approaching a roundabout, seven cars back. It was bustling, and the man in the car in front of us, the sixth car back, had had enough. He got out of his car and walked up to the roundabout. When there was a small gap, he walked into the middle of the roundabout and held up his hand to stop the traffic from the right. Then he waved the first five cars out onto the roundabout; we could not move as his car was in front of us. He then returned to his car, but the roundabout was again busy. We laughed because he now had to wait for the roundabout to be clear for him to move out. There is a saying, 'Patience is a virtue. Possess it if you can. Seldom in a woman, but never in a man'. Er, no offence meant!

In one driving lesson, we had a bizarre occurrence. We came to a roundabout, signalling and positioning to the left. I noticed a blue car next to us, which I assumed was turning right, as the car was in the right-hand lane. So we turned left and went into a small estate to do some manoeuvring. While parked on the left, the same car came up behind us, and after parking up, a woman got out of it, shouting at us and banging on the nearside door window, which I opened a crack.

"You've just hit my car!" she screamed.

"What!" I replied in disbelief. "And where did this supposedly happen?" I asked.

"On the roundabout, over there," she screamed again.

"I don't think so," I quipped.

I was angry but amused.

"I've got proof," she then announced.

"OK, show me," I said.

I got out of my car, and she said, "Look there," pointing to the nearside wing of her car. "There's red paint scraped on my car. The colour of your car," she triumphantly said.

I looked at the wing of her vehicle, but there were no paint marks.

"I can't see any red paint," I replied, unamused.

"Well, it was there a minute ago, and my dad saw it and told me to come and find you," she shouted.

"OK," I said. "Let's look at my car to see if there are any blue marks on it," her car colour.

There were no blue marks. She had children in her vehicle and started accusing my pupil and me of dangerous driving and saying I did not care about her children. I smirked, could not help it, and told her she was *having a laugh* and wondered if we were on Candid Camera, but no, this was real. I had to cut it short before it got too out of hand and got back in my car, and she just stood there on the pavement glaring at us. My pupil was in fits of laughter and loved my telling her she was having a laugh. I heard nothing else from the incident and gladly did not see her on the road again.

I have seen a few episodes by the public, but one comes to mind especially. A black cab driver was so incensed by the driver in front of him in a queue of traffic. He got out of his cab, jumped up and down on the poor man's car bonnet, returned to his taxi and drove off furiously. Clearly, they had a row, but did he need to go that far? Wouldn't like to be in his taxi!

People have mixed feelings about speed humps, but they are there for a reason which is to slow traffic down. However, one of my girls on her test went over a speed hump so fast that the examiner and I hit our heads on the car's roof. It was like a scene out of 'The Dukes of Hazzard'. So she failed her test on awareness. Unfortunately, the council went too far, putting speed humps and mini-roundabouts down an extremely long road through a housing estate. As there were so many of them, the examiners could not use the road any longer because it took far too long to drive through. The council even put humps in the lay-bys where the householders parked their cars! Good thinking!

Sometimes when arriving at a pupil's house, I am told they are still in bed or have just dragged themselves out. Even if their lesson was in the afternoon! I would give them the benefit of the doubt and wait for them, but only give them the remaining time for the lesson. Then if it happened again, I would charge for the lesson, enjoy the time off and not bother with them any longer.

However, the worst pupil I had was when a mother paid for a block of lessons for her son. At first, he was eager to learn, but his attitude changed after his mother paid for another set of lessons. It began when his mother had to start work earlier and left him to his own devices. First, he would still be in bed while I rang the doorbell several times before he appeared. Then he would want to stop at McDonald's and get breakfast or cut the lesson short. I kept threatening to speak with his mum, but it fell on deaf ears until I had enough and directed him to where his mum worked.

"Why have you got me to drive here?" he asked.

"I told you I was going to have a word with your mum, so I rang her to let her know we were coming so she could come out of work to speak to me," I replied.

"Oh, no, that's not fair!" he shouted.

"Well, I warned you, and you took no notice, so here we are," I said.

As his mum approached the car, he got edgy. I got out of the car, went over to her, and explained what had happened. She told him to get out of the car, and they had a blazing row. Finally, she was so angry with him that she told me to leave him there, and he could walk home! Later she rang me and thanked me for letting her know what had been going on, but would I finish the course with him, after which he would pay for lessons himself. He behaved until the end of the course, but I refused to continue with him because of his unreliability. Rightly or wrongly, I assumed he would slip back into his old ways once he took responsibility for paying for his lessons. Later, I learned other instructors had taken him on and got rid of him, and then much later, when teaching a friend of his, I discovered he had passed his test and had crashed his car within a week. So I was pleased I had ended the lessons when I did.

If I had a £1 for all the swearing in the car by my pupils, I could have retired years ago. If directed at themselves for making a mistake, that was not so bad. I usually got a "Sorry, Brenda," so I ignored it, but I would step in if they showed road rage to other drivers.

Road rage is unacceptable by you and other drivers. It can be dangerous! You do not know the attitude of the other driver you are angry with, and they may retaliate and become more aggressive. If another driver is hostile, you must stay calm and uninvolved. A passenger with you could take details of the other vehicle by taking a photograph getting the registration number and make and model. If you are on your own, try and remember the details. Let them pass you by getting out of their way when safe; hopefully, they will drive away. If they don't, keep calm and drive safely. If you are stationary, lock your doors and keep windows shut. Later, when you have calmed down and wish to pursue it, make more detailed notes from what is remembered and notify the police.

One woman I had the misfortune to teach was abusive and loud in verbally expressing herself. She used every swear word known to humanity, whether it was her fault or the other driver's. It was unpleasant for me, and after three lessons, I got rid of her as I did not want to be the one to put her on the road. I remember a cartoon on television around the late 1950s or early 60s. There was a man called Mr Wheeler, and when he left his house in the morning, he was charming and polite, tipping his hat to his neighbours. However, when he got into his car and started driving, he became a red-faced monster, shouting and abusing other drivers and whoever got in his way. When he finally reached his workplace and got out of his car, he became a polite man again. So when they made this cartoon back then, it shows road rage has been around for several years. So if something or someone annoys you, do not retaliate and forget it. It is not worth sending up your heart rate and blood pressure.

I've also had several pupils who have commented on elderly drivers. One said he believed people aged sixty and over should not be driving! Really, how astute of him! However, I took this as a compliment as he did not realise how old his instructor was! See GOV.UK - Bold new measures to keep people safe on the roads.

Unfortunately, some people assume things will go their way. One woman, whose test was in the morning, bought a car and scheduled to collect it in the afternoon. When she told me, I said I did not think it was a good idea because she was putting too much pressure on herself. She sadly failed the test but still had to collect the car. However, her husband drove it home. Waiting for her second attempt was not long, and she passed. This lady could not get on with driving in shoes of any kind, and there are no laws against driving in bare feet, socks, tights, etc., as long as you can completely control the vehicle. (At the time of writing). I also had a lad who would get in the car and lop his shoes onto the back seat, as did a couple of girls I taught. Oppositely, I had a girl who would drive in Dr Marten's boots. I do not know how she managed it, but she could use the pedals without a problem. I tried to get her to drive in regular shoes, but it did not work. So she took her test wearing the boots and passed.

I have taught a few gay lads to drive, one in particular I remember. It was a moment of the adage *'Please floor open up and swallow me'*. I was running late on lessons, and I asked my lad if he would not mind if we could finish at my next pupil's house and for her to drive him home, and he did not object. So we picked her up and explained I was running late. I apologised for him being in the back and asked if she wanted to drive now or when we got to his house. She said she did not mind having a try with a passenger. Then, as she was driving, she started talking about gay men.

She said, "You know what I mean, Brenda, a right-handbag job!"

"Er, I don't know," I replied. "Shall we change the subject? How's your week been since I saw you last? Did you buy that new sofa you wanted?"

"Oh, yes," she said. Then, she explained the delivery and how it looked in her living room.

I glanced slightly to the back of the car to see if he was alright. He looked utterly oblivious to what she said. We arrived at his house, and after he got out of the car, we drove off, and I told her he was gay.

"Oh, no!" she exclaimed. "How embarrassing."

I think more for her than him, and neither said anything in their few following lessons. Then my lady told me she had gone to get her son's new school uniform. When she went into the menswear department in the local clothes shop, she came face to face with my lad. She told me she had apologised and asked him to have a drink with her to make up for it. So he did, and they became great friends, often going out for a drink and a chat. Well, that was a happy ending!

I am embarrassed to say I picked up a couple of parking tickets and a speeding fine as an instructor. But hey-ho, no one's perfect! On two occasions, for parking tickets, I blame my son! The first time we were going Christmas shopping and arguing about something as I was parking up. We were still arguing as we walked out of the car park, and it was not until we were in Marks & Sparks that I remembered I had not paid the car park fee. So yes, I got a ticket. The second time I parked in the car park belonging to his block of flats, and on getting out of my car, I saw people entering them, so I called out for them to hold the door for me, which they did. I spent a couple of hours with my son and then, having to get home, made my way down to my car and found a parking ticket on the windscreen. I rang his intercom.

"I've got a parking ticket!" I shouted at him.

"Oh, yeah," he said, laughing. "Forgot to remind you. You now need a visitor's ticket."

"Well, why didn't you remind me? Since I've been with you for the past two hours!" I angrily exclaimed. "I did not need one before!"

He insisted he had told me and my husband, but we did not remember, and a few months had passed since I had been at his flat. Was I cross, or was I cross? £60 fine! I thought, right, I am going to appeal! But, unfortunately, they had taken a photo of my car, with my driving school name and 'L' plates glaring out. There was also a prominent notice about parking tickets above it, and it was on the Internet! Of course, all my family were bent up with laughter, though I did not think it was funny.

At the time of writing, I had been on the road for 56 years and am pleased to say I had no speeding tickets until one day when I was late for a lesson. I was coming out of a 60 mph limit zone into a 30 mph area, slowing down, but not soon enough to avoid picking up a ticket. The letter came through on my birthday, and opening it, the first words I saw were 'Criminal Record'. Well, what a lovely birthday present! What annoyed me the most was I had not seen the speed camera and could not think where it was, but that was no excuse. I did not take the speed awareness course; too ashamed. So I paid the fine and got three points on my licence, which I am pleased to say are now spent.

CHAPTER SIX

NEAR AND ACTUAL ACCIDENTS

AN ANECDOTE FROM A COLLEAGUE'S PUPIL...

Instructor – "What would you have done if that pedestrian had walked out in front of you?" Pupil – "Hit them!"

FACT – 2.5 million vehicles were on Britain's roads in 1934, and 7,343 people were killed in road accidents. By 2004, there were 30 million vehicles on the road, with 3,221 deaths. Lord Leslie Hore-Belisha said, "Driving is an art in which those who are engaged should, in the interest of their own and of the public's safety, take the greatest pains to make themselves proficient." The yellow flashing globe at a Zebra crossing is called a Belisha beacon, named after Lord Leslie Hore-Belisha, who introduced it in 1934. The first beacon was erected on the southern edge of Hyde Park on Kensington Road.

I have always believed in God, and I am sure he has a guardian angel looking after me. The saying 'There, but for the grace of God, go I' is very true. I have often driven to a pupil's house and used the same route, with the pupil driving 10 to 15 minutes later, to find there had been an accident.

My guardian angel was definitely with me when driving to a lesson, and a Ford Fiesta was coming in the opposite direction. It was a country road but wide enough for two cars to pass each other safely. I suddenly realised that the Ford Fiesta kept the same speed and headed straight for me. My instinct came in, and I swung the car onto a high bank of grass on my left, and we missed each other by inches. The Ford Fiesta did not stop, obviously wanting to escape the situation. It happened so quickly there was no time to get the registration number. The driver might have been texting or talking on their mobile or falling asleep. It could have turned into a severe accident if I had not had the grass bank on the left with no bushes or trees. I had to calm myself for the next lesson and wondered what would have happened if one of my pupils had been driving. Best not to think about it!

Then there was the time when we were heading towards a long bend with four cars approaching us. An impatient driver overtook the four oncoming cars while negotiating it, aiming at us. I went to grab the steering wheel to pull us onto the grass bank on the left (thank goodness for grass banks) when the oncoming vehicle had the same idea, going up onto the bank to pass us. My pupil and I were shaken up, but I had to hide my feelings and find a safe place to stop to console and calm her since her driving test was in an hour. Fortunately, she got herself together and, being a competent driver, passed the first time.

There was an occasion when I am sure a child's guardian angel was with her. I was explaining to Ingrid, my pupil, the dangers of heavily parked vehicles; for example, pedestrians, elderly people, children stepping out, prams being pushed out, etc., when it happened! A child stepped out from behind a parked car, thankfully well ahead of us. Ingrid emergency stopped, but it was as though someone got hold of the child's shoulders and pulled her back. The mother was strapping the baby into the car seat, not realising her toddler had gone behind the car.

"That was weird. What do you think happened there?" Ingrid asked worriedly.

"Don't know," I said. "Maybe it was the child's guardian angel looking after her."

"Well, I didn't believe in guardian angels, but I do now," she replied with an amazed look. Unfortunately, by the time we had gathered ourselves and for me to let the mother know what had happened, she had driven off, unaware of the situation. She should have put the toddler in the car to keep her safe while strapping the baby in.

The most embarrassing accident was when we hit another learner's car. We were in a village with narrow roads. I asked my pupil to turn left at the end of the road, and as she turned, she went onto the accelerator instead of the footbrake. Unfortunately, I missed my footbrake, so we hit the learner's car, approaching the junction to turn right. Luckily, I knew the instructor, and we exchanged details, sorting out the sticky wicket.

"Are you literally teaching your pupils how to crash a car?" he chuckled.

"Er, yes, sorry about that. But didn't you know it is on the new curriculum where we have to teach our learners in real-time what to do if they crash their car?" I said, trying to diffuse the situation.

"Wait until I tell the others you're doing actual crash courses now," he jokingly replied.

"OK, OK, don't rub it in," I remorsefully said.

I have had a few rear shunts, with the driver behind not focusing correctly, not realising we had not moved off, or being impatient. Even with 'L' plates, caution notices and asking drivers to be patient displayed on the back of the car, the rear shunts still happened. Some have been minor and easily dealt with, but others have been serious, with the car going in for repair. One time (as I look back, I can see the funny side of it, but I did not then), I was running late for a lesson. My lady pupil agreed for me to pick up my next lady on the way home to her house, which was a short distance away (both of them were in their late 50s), with my next lady sitting in the back. We were waiting at a roundabout (where most rear shunts happen) when a lorry behind us moved off before we did and walloped us. The rear window exploded, with glass flying everywhere, and it knocked the chassis out of position, frightening us all. However, the funny side was the name of the company the driver worked for. It was called *'Wreckers International'*. He certainly did an excellent job with my car! My ladies showed true grit by keeping up their lessons and passing their driving tests. But unfortunately, one of them was involved in another minor accident. She was practising the turn-in-the-road manoeuvre and went too fast when on the first leg to drive the car across the road. I again missed my footbrake, and we went straight into a wooden garden gate! An elderly lady and gentleman cautiously opened their front door and peered out. I went over to them, frantically apologising.

"I am so, so sorry. It wasn't my learner driver's fault. But, unfortunately, it was me. I missed my footbrake when I knew she wasn't using hers," I ashamedly said.

They were kind to me, saying, "Don't worry, my dear, no harm done."

"But I've broken the lock on your gate. So I will pay for it to be repaired," I replied.

"No, don't worry about it," they kindly said.

But I insisted, got a trades-person to repair it and paid for it.

One of my girls, Jessica, passed her test the first time and had been on the road for a few months when she telephoned me, saying she had got eight points on her licence and had to retake her tests. She had already retaken and passed the theory but now needed refresher lessons for the practical. I felt so sorry for her, even more so when Jessica told me what had happened. She had turned right onto a side road and felt a bump but thought nothing of it until the police knocked on her door, saying she had not stopped at the scene of an accident.

"I was so scared. I couldn't understand how it happened because there was no oncoming traffic when I turned right, so I thought I was safe," Jessica said.

"So, what did you think the bump was?" I asked.

"I just thought I had gone into a dip in the road, and the car bumped its way out of it," she explained.

However, the bump Jessica felt was a motorbike clipping the rear of her car as she was entering the side road.

We often practised this junction in her lessons because she would frequently use it to get home once she had passed her test. It was before a blind bend at least 100 yards away, clear, and on a 30 mph limit road. So, she was safe to turn as far as she was concerned. Unfortunately, it went to court, and they revoked her licence. She was distraught and adamant it was clear before making the turn and could only think the bike rider was speeding, but it was not considered. Undeterred and showing her bravery, she re-took her practical test and again passed the first time.

A colleague was on a lesson and came to crossroads to crossover to the opposite side. His pupil stopped to check the junction and, as far as they were concerned, although there was a car approaching from the left, knew it was safe and had time to cross. However, as they proceeded, my colleague noticed the car from the left had deliberately sped up, aiming for them. He yelled at his pupil to go faster, but it was too late, and the speeding driver hit the nearside rear of his car. It went to court, but my colleague lost the case as the judge said he had unsafely crossed the path of another vehicle. He was furious that the judge would think he would have allowed his pupil to cross the other driver's path without considering the car's speed. Unfortunately, there were no witnesses to corroborate his account of the situation.

Apart from an earlier story of a near head-on collision when driving to pupils' driving test. A couple of other pupils have also been involved in an accident on their way to their test. We were on a 30 mph dual carriageway and slowing down to give way at a roundabout when the driver behind hit us. I saw the car in my mirror, and it was slowing down, but not enough to stop safely behind us! Luckily, it was only the tail light cover broken, and the lights still worked. But, unfortunately, it cost my lady (who you will read about in the '*Dreams' c*hapter*)* her test because she was too upset by it.

Another time was when it was pouring rain, and we were stationary in a queue of traffic. I looked in my mirror and saw a car coming up from behind, not letting up speed.

"Brace yourself. We're going to be hit!" I exclaimed to Grace.

Before she could reply, the car banged straight into the back of my car.

"Oh no. I've got my test in half an hour. Can I still do it?" Grace pleaded.

"I'm going to check the back, and if nothing vital is broken, it should go ahead," I reassured her.

The driver got out of her car, stunned, and said, "I am so sorry, I am so sorry," but I made her feel guilty by telling her we were going to my pupil's driving test. Well, these things have to be said! Luckily, my car was still roadworthy, and the test went ahead, but Grace also failed because although she wanted to still do the test, it unnerved her. But passed on the next attempt.

FACT – It is generally not your fault if someone hits you from behind. A basic rule of the road requires a driver to stop their vehicle safely if traffic is stationary ahead.

The safest way to judge a gap is to use the two-second rule. So, in good weather, keep a minimum of a two-second gap between you and the vehicle in front. Double the gap in poor weather, four seconds, and ten times the stopping distance in icy weather. This gives you time and space to react to any problems ahead. See stopping distances in the Highway Code. When I asked one of my pupils what rule they followed to keep a safe distance from the vehicle in front of them in good weather, they answered the two-minute rule! Er, no. Drivers have enough trouble keeping the two-second rule, let alone two minutes!

The way to carry out this rule is just as the vehicle in front passes a fixed point, such as a road sign, lamp post or a bridge, begin saying, 'Only a fool breaks the two-second rule', at a steady rate. The phrase takes about two seconds, so if you pass the fixed point before you have finished saying it, you are too close and should leave more room. If you want to be cheery, you could also say, 'One pink elephant, two pink elephants'!

There have been a few other occasions when another vehicle has hit us. Still, one time I had to keep myself calm and collected as I knew the (sorry to say) elderly man had begun lying to me. We were in a queue of traffic approaching a roundabout when the driver behind hit us. I got out of the car with a notepad, ready to take his details, but he insisted he had not hit me. Eventually, he got out of his car to look and then agreed that he had.

He said, "If you pull over to the left, we can sort this out."

He made me suspicious, so I refused to move and he accused me of holding up the traffic. I knew what was on his mind. If I pulled over, he would drive off. I asked him for his name and address, but I knew he was lying because of how he acted and spoke. So, after I went to the back of his car to take down the registration number and the make and model, he told me he had been telling 'porkies' (lying). He gave me his real name and address and also his insurance details. There was no point in lying now as I had his car's registration number and make and model.

Remember, you must stand your ground if asked to pull over to exchange details because the offender will probably drive off and leave you with maybe a hefty bill on your hands. This happened to a friend of mine. Do not worry about holding up traffic, as other drivers will get around you, and sometimes you may also have a witness to what has happened. When I got home, I reported the incident to my insurance company. I also reported it to the police if anything came of it.

FACT – After an accident, legally, all concerned should safely stop at the scene.

- **Switch on the hazard warning lights.**
- **Call the police and an ambulance if there is an injury to anyone.**
- **All involved should exchange the following details:-**
- **Name, address and telephone number.**
- **Name, address of their insurance company and the policy number.**
- **Their driving licence number.**
- **Make, model and colour of the vehicles.**
- **The registration number of the vehicles.**

- **Witnesses, if possible.**
- **Call the police if the road is blocked.**

It is also a good idea to take a photograph of the damage. You must report the accident to your insurance company within 24 hours of the accident. For more information if an accident happens, go to GOV.UK/Vehicle Insurance.

I would give dual carriageway lessons to pupils, teaching them how to enter, exit and overtake when necessary; without breaking the speed limit. Rob, who I was teaching, had overtaken several vehicles, going through the drill of mirrors, shoulder checking and signalling. However, I could see he was becoming impulsive by starting to glimpse the mirrors. I checked my mirror when he began overtaking another vehicle, and I saw a car hurtling down the carriageway behind us, travelling at least 100 mph, if not more. I grabbed the steering wheel, and we swerved back into the left lane like a swinging pendulum as the car passed us. We both went quiet, realising it could have been a severe accident.

"Whew, that was a near miss!" I exclaimed.

It startled him, and he said, "Brenda, I saw the car, but I thought I had enough time to overtake and get back in."

"I know you did, but it was a glimpse, which didn't give you enough time to judge the speed and distance of the car," I explained. "You were getting into a habit of going through the motions of checking and not taking in properly what you were seeing. You've got to be on the ball all the time."

An older lady, I taught, putting it politely, was v-e-r-r-y challenging. I concluded she should not be on the road when the following happened. We attempted to cross a dual carriageway from a side road to the opposite side. It was staggered, so we had to turn left onto the carriageway, right into a central reservation, and then cross over to the other side. I explained what she had to do, but she must have been in panic mode and only heard me say, "Right"! So, when the first section of the carriageway was clear, I told her to go. Instead of turning left, she turned right into the face of the oncoming traffic. Although the traffic was initially far enough away and safe for us to enter the carriageway, it was getting closer as she tried to turn right. I grabbed the steering wheel to pull us back to the left, but she had a firm grip. I screamed at her to let go of the wheel and got ourselves to the left. The traffic was getting nearer and nearer, and the drivers began hooting aggressively! This was a split-second scenario. My life did not even have time to flash before my eyes! At the end of the lesson, we had a long chat about what had happened. She said she felt disorientated about the road layout. As confusion had set in at other times when I had to explain the more straightforward road layouts, we both concluded that driving was not for her and finished the lessons.

Another life-threatening situation occurred on another dual carriageway. Like the previous story, we needed to cross the dual carriageway from a side road. We did not need to get into the central reservation directly ahead of us as this was for the oncoming traffic to use when turning right off the dual carriageway and for traffic turning right from the side road. We just needed to turn left and go over two lanes to the slip road next to the central reservation. I explained what needed to be done to my lad, and he said he understood. When it was clear, he drove across the two lanes, but instead of going into the slip lane, he went into the central reservation. OK, I thought, he's going to turn right. Still, noooo, he turned left into the slip lane facing the oncoming traffic, who wanted to turn right off the dual carriageway! It happened so quickly that I did not have time to use my dual controls to stop him. This must have been our lucky day, as no oncoming traffic wanted to turn right. But the hand gestures and shouting from other drivers are unprintable. The atmosphere in the car was intense, and you can probably guess what I said to him. This story and the previous one. Also, the Ford Fiesta and the oncoming car overtaking vehicles on a bend are equally number one on my list of hair-raising situations!

One dark evening I turned into a junction, and I realised just in time that there was a rope across the road, about 3ft up from it. Whoever had tied one end to a lamppost and the other to a fence. I stopped as it was just about to hit the headlamps of my car. I looked around to see who was about, not wanting to leave the car. An elderly lady and gentleman were walking along the road and saw me. I felt more comfortable getting out of the car when they approached me and asked if I was alright. We were looking around, and whoever had tied the rope across the road was nowhere to be seen. Luckily, I had a pair of scissors in my car and cut the rope. Whoever did this, thinking it was funny, needed to have their brains tested, as it was the worst stupidest thing to do. If it had been a motorbike rider or a cyclist, they could have come off their bikes and possibly killed. I reported it to the police, who said they would investigate. I hope they did.

While driving in a local town during rush hour, a builder's truck was behind us with two men and a boy. It was a 30 mph limit road, but the driver was extraordinarily impatient and continuously tried to overtake us. We finally arrived at a big roundabout above a motorway, signalling to turn right and taking up the position. As we moved onto the roundabout, the truck driver, now on our left, swung into our nearside deliberately. I sounded the horn several times, and he pulled over on the left, after which I came up behind him, keeping a distance.

"He deliberately hit us!" Heather, my pupil, shouted. "What a moron! Why did he do that?"

"Well, I'd better have a word with him. Probably he's going to tell me how to do my job, and we've got no right to be on the road," I replied wearily.

He got out of the truck, and I went to him, ready to take details. As predicted, he told me I had no right to be on the road with a learner at this time of night (5.30 pm) and, to boot, even in the evening rush hour. He wanted to know the name of my pupil, but I refused to give it to him and took down the registration number and make of the truck. He kept asking for my pupil's name, which I refused to give him, so he threatened to call the police. I told him to go ahead, but he kept arguing, and I said I did not care if he called the police. Finally, he did and went back to his truck. When the police officer arrived, I was standing beside my car, and he came to me first. I told him what had happened but had no proof of who had hit who because there were no witnesses. I also informed him of the truck driver, saying I had no right to be on the road, to which he said,

"Well, that's his opinion!"

He took my details and then went over to him. I could see the truck driver was irate. The officer got him to do a breathalyser test, which was negative - what a shame! Then the officer breathalysed my pupil. I was expecting him to breathalyse me, but he said he did not need to because of a loophole in the law (at that point in time), meaning I could have been over the limit! What a pity because I wanted to have a go! Well, I like to try things out. The police officer confirmed my details to him and his to me. However, it did not put my pupil off; she passed her test the first time. I had it in my mind to post him a pile of dog poo, but I thought it best not to!

An open-topped box lorry came towards us when Pat, one of my pupils, drove back from the test area. It was carrying planks of wood standing on end. Suddenly there was a big gust of wind, and it took a plank up into the air, heading straight towards us.

"Ohhhh, we're going to die!" screeched Pat.

"No, we're not," I said, praying it would go over the top of us.

I grabbed the steering wheel as we had nowhere to go. If we had swerved to the right, we would have had a head-on collision with the oncoming lorry. There was a ditch filled with water to the left, and we could not stop because we had vehicles behind us. We were both cowering down in our seats, watching this plank of wood flying towards us, but by the grace of God, it hit the car's roof and fell down the back of it, and the vehicle behind ran over it.

"*That* was a near miss! Somebody is looking after us today," I said with great relief. "Are you OK, Pat? Do you still want to drive?"

"I'm OK, apart from shaking. I'll be alright to drive home," Pat replied timidly.

"You sure?" I queried.

"Yes, I am sure," this brave woman replied.

Was my guardian angel with me again?

Pat was in her middle 50s and treated it as just one of those things when we discussed it later. She was going through the menopause and having day and night sweats. When I picked her up for her first test, she was in a bit of a state, which is enough to make you sweat anyway, but in the middle of her test, she had a menopausal sweat with droplets running down her face. The male examiner did not realise what was happening; they had seen enough sweaty people on their tests before. I had to give her credit because she carried on with the test regardless but did not make it. I went out with her for the second attempt without problems, and she passed.

Also, a similar situation to the plank of wood happened to my friend's husband when driving on a motorway. A metal sheet headed towards his car from the opposite side of the carriageway. He was braking and had the good sense to unbuckle his seat belt and lay on the passenger seat as the metal sheet went through the windscreen and out of the rear window. Had he not done so, he may have been decapitated!

My family and I were on a journey to Nottingham, and my husband was in the third lane, overtaking traffic. On the road before us, two bicycles had fallen off the back of a car. He shouted, "Hang on" while swerving into the second lane where, thankfully, it was clear. I hate to think about what happened behind us when other cars approached the bikes. So these three stories show the importance of securing your load carefully and tightly. Otherwise, you could cause a serious accident. You can find more information on GOV.UK Driver Vehicle and Standards Agency – Vehicle loading.

Sometimes you r-e-a-l-l-y cannot believe your eyes are seeing what they are seeing. For example, approaching a mini-roundabout, two teenagers, a boy and a girl, were sitting in the middle of a mini-roundabout with their backs together and arms interlocked. We pulled up just before them, and I got out of my car to ask what they were doing.

"What does it look like?" was the answer from the boy.

"Do you think it's a good idea sitting here like this? "Do you want to be killed if another driver doesn't see you in time?" I retorted.

"Oh, we want to see what people do when they see us. It's funny," he said, with both of them now laughing.

"I'm calling the police, then we'll see if you think it's funny," I replied.

"Do what you like. We don't care," the boy cockily replied and swore at me.

I got back into the car and got my pupil to turn left at the mini-roundabout, so we could park up and for me to ring the police. We then noticed a man in another car had stopped and was talking to them. Whatever he said to them made them get up and move on. However, I still notified the police as they may have pulled the prank at another mini-roundabout. Was this some stupid dare thing?

During a lesson, we approached a wheelie bin near the grass verge (no pavement). I said to Lucy, my pupil, "Mind the wheelie bin, Lucy, please," trying to let her know she needed to move out slightly to miss it.

"Lucy, mind the wheelie bin," I urgently repeated.

She was making no effort to avoid it, so I quickly pushed the steering wheel away, but to no avail. So, yes, we hit it and broke the nearside mirror.

"What were you thinking?" I asked.

"The wheelie bin must have rolled forward into my way!" was her reply.

"What an excuse, and no, I somehow don't think so," I replied in exasperation. "It's you not judging the distance between you and the bin."

That was the end of the lesson I intended to do, as we had to drive into town to get a new mirror. However, a couple of weeks later, we were on the same road and guess what was at the side of the road this time? A washing machine in the same place as the wheelie bin!

"Mind the washing machine," I said. "You don't want to go home and tell your family you hit a washing machine; they'd never believe you."

She did not hit it, but I was out on a lesson with her brother driving along a narrow country road. We had to swerve to the left to miss a fast oncoming vehicle. Regrettably, there was a branch in the hedgerow which needed to be cut back further, and yes, the nearside mirror got it again. About ten other mirrors were on the floor when I got out of the car to see if I could retrieve it, so plenty of other drivers had lost their mirror. I was waiting for it to happen again. However, the adage of things coming in threes did not occur. Well, not until a few years later when another pupil hit a wheelie bin and broke the mirror again.

Driving around an estate, Amanda turned onto a side road. As we passed a driveway, a car quickly started backing out without looking to see if anything was coming.

"Quick, accelerate," I shouted to her, but the driver still caught the offside rear of my car. We stopped, and I got out of my car and went over to the car driver who had hit us and found it was an elderly lady. I knocked on the nearside window and told her she had just hit my car.

"Oh, dear," she said. "I thought it was a brick that I went over!"

"Er, no," I said. "It was my car!"

"Don't worry, my dear, I'll get my husband, and we'll sort out the insurance," she replied.

Then she went indoors. She and her husband came out, and we exchanged details, and he scolded her for not wearing her glasses! But I could not get angry with them because they were such a sweet couple. I thought, however, her driving leaves much to be desired, and perhaps it was time for her to consider giving it up.

Sometimes it did not sink in, no matter what I told specific learners of both sexes, mainly boys, about being a careful driver. The attitude was, "Oh, that won't happen to me." I would try to instil in them how they would feel if they killed someone or maimed them, but unfortunately, they still did not take it on board. For instance, teaching two lads, who were friends, to drive, there was a lot of banter between them about who would pass first and who would have the first accident. One of them was spending a lot of money adapting his car and saying he gave his friend six months before he had an accident.

"Really," I said. "I give you three!"

"That won't happen," he retorted. "I love my car and spent a lot of money on it, so I won't smash it up."

However, he was the first to do so and within the time limit I had stated. The other one bragged about how many cars he had smashed up. He worked for a tyre company I used and took great delight in telling me about it when he served me. I was unimpressed and told him so, hoping he would realise his stupidity one day.

People thinking about learning to drive must decide how they will learn. Either in the conventional way, a semi-intensive course or a one-week crash course.

Most people choose to learn conventionally, where you usually have one or two weekly lessons, because of affordability and the time they can spare. It also has the enabling advantage of thinking things through during the week. A semi-intensive course spread over one, two, or three months will allow you to learn faster and have the advantage of time to ponder. These two ways of learning also help to read the road (hazard perception) more substantially because of being able to drive elsewhere other than perhaps only driving around the test area.

A one-week crash course is highly intensive in usually having five hours of driving per day for five, six or seven days, and possibly not giving you the advantage to mull things over because of tiredness. Also, you might only learn in the test area, which may not show you the benefit of hazard perception when driving in other places. If you decide on a one-week crash course, gaining some knowledge of car controls and passing the theory test is better. Always remember the DVSA's slogan is 'Safe Driving for Life'.

I had a lady who took a one-week crash course and passed her test. She found it challenging to drive independently because it scared her, as she found it hard to hazard percept while driving in strange areas; she only focused on the road layout. Eventually, she had a terrible accident. She had refresher lessons with me practising in different places, and gradually her confidence and hazard perception grew. After she left me, I hoped she kept relaxed and enjoyed driving.

It is good when the police are in the right place at the right time (although I have moaned about them before) and see someone doing something mindless, such as when approaching a red traffic light and the driver behind overtaking us and jumping it. The driver obviously had not checked the mirrors because right behind him was a police car. So they chased and pulled the driver over before he could get onto the dual carriageway. Of course, we cracked up laughing.

On another occasion, an articulated lorry overtook us on a mini-roundabout. We swerved up onto the pavement and nearly hit a fence and tree.

"Why the hell did he do that?" Jenny cried out. "He scared the living daylights out of me."

"The fearful and worrying thing is, if the lorry driver carries on doing brainless things like that, he will kill himself and take someone else with him," I said.

We then heard sirens coming from behind us and, as luck would have it, a police officer on his motorbike, seeing what had happened, chased after and stopped him.

Another occurrence when the police were spot on time was when we were being followed by a car within a 30 mph limit, constantly trying to overtake us. Similar to the builder's truck, as mentioned above. We turned left at the end of the road, and the driver overtook us (still on the 30 mph limit road) and drove straight towards a speed check camera. The police officer could see what had happened and had a big smile. I put my thumb up and mouthed, 'Thank you'.

As Lord Leslie Hore-Belisha quoted in the Fact above, "Drivers must take pains to be proficient to keep themselves and others safe."

CHAPTER SEVEN

BREAKDOWNS

AN ANECDOTE FROM A COLLEAGUE'S PUPIL...

My pupil, "If this car breaks down, can you drive me home?" Me, "Er, no. How can I if my car breaks down?" Pupil, "Oh, yeah, you won't be able to."

When I started teaching, cars were less efficient and reliable than today, and I have had my fair share of breakdowns. For example, it was pouring rain and test day for one of my girls. I went with her as she needed moral support. She was driving nicely, and all was going well until the engine made a loud noise.

"Oh noooo," I thought. "Please don't break down."

Realising there was a problem, my pupil calmly said to the examiner.

"There appears to be something wrong with the car!"

Then, it came to a grinding halt, luckily next to a telephone box and me being with her. The examiner said professionally,

"Don't worry, my dear. I'll leave you with your instructor to sort it out."

In this disastrous situation, nothing was left but for the examiner to walk back to the test centre. It was about a quarter of a mile away and still pouring rain! I called out my fourth emergency service, my husband, to tow me home (actually, I remember him having to tow me many times). So as it was my fault, I paid for her next test and gave her free lessons leading up to it.

On another occasion, my car downed tools while driving up a hill. There was a long queue of traffic behind, but a man kindly got out of his car to see if he could help. Just a few feet up the road was an entrance to a quarry, and I asked him if he could push us up to it. So he and Gail, my pupil, pushed while I steered the car into the entrance. Nobody else got out of their vehicles to help, which I thought was unsporting, but I was oh-so grateful to the man who helped us. As the fourth emergency service was unavailable, Gail and I walked down the drive to the quarry office to ask if I could use their telephone. We had to take a bit of stick off the men, thinking they were funny taking the mickey out of us two women, but they let me use their telephone to ring the garage for us to be towed to my house.

During another lesson, my car made a loud noise. I saw the fan belt had broken off when I looked in my mirror and lying in the middle of the road. The car behind was hooting us, and I put my hand up to let him know I knew what was going on.

"Oh, flipping heck, the fan belt has broken," I told my pupil Sarah.

I looked at the temperature gauge, it had already gone up, and we were a couple of miles from my house.

"We're going to have to stop because the engine is overheating," I said.

Luckily, there was a lay-by where we could pull in.

"We can only drive a few yards before the temperature gauge goes up," I said. "When it does, we'll have to stop and let the engine cool down."

"Um, I foresee a lot of vehicles hooting us," Sarah said philosophically and laughing. At least she could see the funny side of it. We carried on driving, stopping each time the temperature gauge went up. The vehicles behind us became impatient because we held them up and stopped inconveniently. But we grinned and bore it. However, it made an exciting lesson for Sarah, learning what to do if the car overheats when the fan belt breaks. I doubt, though, *she* would do what we did!

I bought a new car and was in the first lesson with a new pupil. Unfortunately, as she started driving, the tailgate hoisted itself of its own accord.

"What's going on?" Mandy asked. "This is creepy!"

"Er, I don't know," I replied. "Perhaps I didn't shut it properly when I put something in the boot."

After getting her to park up and firmly shutting it, we drove on, but it happened twice more.

"Oh, dear," I said. "I think I've got a problem. It's not catching properly, but no worries. I'll lock the doors and see if that works."

Luckily, it did, and the car had to return to the garage to change the catch. Thankfully, it did not put her off having lessons with me.

I have had the starter motor breakdown twice, but the fourth emergency service came to the rescue. Abigail learnt how to jump-start the car. She and my husband were pushing, and me dealing with the steering and controls. When the starter motor broke down the first time, it was a week before I could get it into the repair garage. So my husband showed me how to keep the car going if it let me down. I let my pupils know and asked if they still wanted a lesson. They all said yes, so out we went, and I prayed they would not stall the car. But, of course, a few did either at the end of a road or at a roundabout. So, I was with the bonnet up, tapping the starter motor, and my pupil was turning the key to start the engine. They thought it was hilarious and had a lesson on how to get the car going again if the starter motor went.

It was about 7 pm and a dark, cold, windy winter's evening. We were driving along a country lane when Nikki, my pupil, hit a pothole and the tyre burst. We limped along to a lay-by and pulled into it. I jacked the car up, and we both had a go at trying to undo the locking nut. But, still being two weak women (ha-ha), we could not get it undone, so I called my husband (luckily, mobiles were in by then), gave him directions to where we were, and he set out to find us.

Meanwhile, I lowered the car off the jack, and we sat in it to keep warm. It was slightly windy, and we heard a tapping sound, which seemed to be on the car.

"What's that noise? Did you hear a tapping?" Nikki whispered. "Er, yes, but it's nothing to worry about," I replied, trying not to sound nervous.

So, we looked around, and nothing was there to cause the tapping. Then it happened again, and she was getting anxious. I was not too fond of it either, but I put on a brave face to keep her calm. After that, the wind increased and started howling around the car, so I can tell you we were both happy when my husband turned up. Later, after telling people what had happened, I was told of ghostly things along that road. I did not take my pupils there in the dark again!

A few years ago, I took on a pupil who had trouble learning to drive and wanted to try again. She was edgy, which can hold pupils back, but she was determined to do it this time. We were driving home along a wide country road. It was about 6 pm, dark and bustling traffic as people travelled from work. We hit a pothole, but the tyre did not burst straight away. We got close to her home, and then it went down. I called the fourth emergency service, and she called her dad to pick her up. She was upset, but I reassured her it was not her fault. She continued learning; however, a few months later, the same thing happened again. This time two tyres burst, so we had to stop. We noticed a car at a farm entrance a few feet up the road opposite us. This same pothole had also caught the driver. We changed seats so I could drive shuffling along the road, looking for a place to pull into. You can imagine the vehicles behind us were building up. Realising our situation, a man standing at the side of the road directed us to a company entrance where two other cars had also hit the pothole. One of them was my ex-pupil, and the man directing us off the road was her boyfriend, whom she had called for help.

Again I telephoned my husband. Luckily, we had two spare tyres, and while waiting for him, another car turned into the entrance with a burst tyre from that irksome pothole. Once more, my poor girl felt devastated, and I had to reassure her again it was not her fault. However, the brave girl continued her lessons without any more problems and passed her test with flying colours.

I reported it to the council on the first occasion, but they were unhelpful and would not reimburse me. The second time I reported it to the council, they tried to dismiss it, but I let my insurance company know. Finally, my insurance company put their solicitors on the case, and the council had to pay. After this, the council took another four years to repair the road, so goodness knows how many other vehicles suffered.

If you do not have a fourth emergency service, I suggest you enrol with one of the breakdown companies. The driving test now includes Show/Tell questions (introduced in December 2017) about basic car maintenance knowledge. You can find the questions on GOV.UK under Car – 'Show me, Tell me' vehicle safety questions.

I bought a new car and used it for about three months. My husband got an urgent telephone call from the garage to say I had to get off the road as I had duplicate registration plates. The way they compensated me was to give me another new car. A few months later, I went to pick up a parcel from someone and noticed the car in their drive was the one I had been using. It had the same registration plates, so the garage had sorted the problem out. When I told the person who owned the car it had been my driving school car, she could not believe her luck. On checking it over, a friend of hers, a car mechanic, said he thought it had been a driving school car as he could see the drill holes where the dual controls had been. She had been arguing with the garage about it being a driving school car because they had sold it to her as a demonstration car. So now she had proof to the contrary, and the garage had to own up to the fact. They offered her another second-hand car, but she wanted a new one. The garage refused, so she took them to court. I advised her to take the car they offered her as she pushed her luck to be given a new one. Sadly, she lost the case as the judge found in favour of the garage, which I thought they would. She had to pay for court costs and keep the car. So she was a great deal out of pocket.

A few years later, a new model of my car came out. The garage mentioned above, had changed hands, so I went to them to trade in my car for the new model. But trouble was again brewing.

I was going to pick up a girl for her driving test, and when I started the engine, I remembered I had forgotten something indoors. So I turned the engine off and went to collect it. When I returned to the car and turned the key, the engine would not start. Panic! My husband tried to get the car going while I telephoned my girl, and she and her dad came to my house. He and my husband had their heads in the engine but could not get it going. So, we had to tow the car to the garage for them to sort it out. After they had the car for a couple of days, I telephoned them to find out what was wrong. They said they could not find the problem, so they took the complete engine out of the car. They did this without my permission and told me it would cost over £2,000 to repair it as the warranty had run out. I was not best pleased. The garage was a dealership of a well-known car manufacturer, so my husband contacted the manufacturer's head office. They investigated the garage to find out why they had done this and sent their engineers to the garage to deal with it.

The manufacturer then got in touch with me to apologise. They gave me one of their demonstration cars and put the dual controls from my car into it. They had my car for three months before it was roadworthy again, and I was putting a lot of mileage on their demonstration car. As for my girl, I compensated her with free lessons, and she took her test in the demonstration car and passed. Even after they had repaired my car, I did not turn the engine off immediately after turning it on, just in case. As you will see in the '*Dreams*' chapter, I had more trouble with this garage.

As a learner's car gains a lot of mileage, I needed to change my car again. There was another new model out, so I decided not to go to the previous garage to buy from them because of my trouble and bought the latest model from a different garage. But, after 5,000 miles, the clutch was wearing out. The garage tried to blame my learners, to which I felt pretty insulted for thinking I would let my learners ride the clutch. However, they put a new one in, but after another 5,000 miles, it happened again. By now, a large driving school in the London area was also having trouble with the clutches wearing out on their cars. On investigation, the problem was the design of the clutch. So until they solved the issue, the clutch had to be changed every 5,000 miles. When the new design was fitted, it lasted over 100,000 miles.

CHAPTER EIGHT

MANOEUVRES

AN ANECDOTE FROM A COLLEAGUE'S PUPIL…

I asked a pupil to reverse into a bay. He looked at me and said, "You want me to reverse backwards?"

As time passed, the driving test developed to include new reverse manoeuvres. One was the 'parallel park'. Using another person's car is generally the only way to practise this manoeuvre. But, sometimes, the car owner would get upset about it, not realising the instructor was in control and would not allow the learner to damage their vehicle. Some owners would come out of their houses and drive off or have loud words with me. I usually came back with the answer to report me to the DVSA, who, I am sorry to say, was not helpful to us driving instructors. When we reported complaints to the DVSA about the public being unhappy, their answer was to knock on the door of the vehicle's owner to get their consent. Yeah, right! So, instead, we put up with abuse from the public while trying to teach our learners how to parallel park.

I taught a friend of my son to drive, and speaking to his mum, she asked what we intended to do in his lesson. I said the parallel park. She told me she had to chase off a driving instructor doing the manoeuvre around her car and hoped I did not use other people's cars to do it. Well, of course, I said I had to. Where or what else could I do? Her answer was to use a skip or something. I did not continue the conversation, as I knew it was not worth it.

"What do you think you are doing?" I was often asked by the public when practising the manoeuvre. When asked if it was their car, they frequently said no. So I would politely ask them to go away! Most would walk off in a huff, but others would try to make something out of nothing.

Practising the manoeuvre around a car, we were halfway through it when the owner came out and took his car across the road to park it. Then, he stormed back to his house with looks that could kill us.

"OK," I said to Gina, my pupil. "Don't let him put us off. I'm going to help you finish the manoeuvre." We were giggling as we brought the car to the kerb with expertise. That showed him!

Another time, a woman was leaving her house on the opposite side of the road. We were not in her way, but she thought so, hooting and shouting at us. After we had finished, she drove out of her driveway and blocked us in. She then got out of her car to write my registration number down.

"What the hell do you think you are doing? I'm reporting you to the police!" she retorted.

"Fair enough," I said. "But you won't get anywhere with it because we have to teach this manoeuvre included in the driving test."

"We'll see about that," she confidently said.

She ranted and raved and finally drove off. Afterwards, I heard no more about it. Why are people so against learners when they were once a learner?

We came alongside another car to do the parallel park, and a voice said,

"Move away from this vehicle!"

We looked about us but saw no one. The voice said again to move away from this vehicle. We still saw no one, and then it said,

"Move away from this vehicle. You have 15 seconds to do so!" Was it going to explode?

So we scarpered quickly but pulled over a little way down the road looking for somebody, but nobody was about. So we concluded it must have been a talking car alarm. Well, it definitely alarmed us!

I had my car washed one day by a kind gentleman. My pupil had just carried out a parallel park, and we were sitting behind the car we had just used to do the manoeuvre. As we discussed the procedure, this gentleman threw a bucket of water over my car. Thankfully, the windows were shut! When I looked out, he hand gestured to me and shouted, "Clear off." As we had used his car, he was unhappy about it. My response was to blow him a kiss!

Listening to the radio a few years ago about an advert for women's car insurance. Two men were sitting in their car watching somebody trying to parallel park.

The conversation was something like, "Cor blimey, look at that. Making a right pig's ear of it. It's got to be a woman. Can't get into that space? It's easy-peasy."

After this person had parked, on getting out of the car, lo-and-behold, it was a man!

So the conversation then turned to something like,

"I think he did well there in that small space. I would've had trouble doing it. Perhaps we should've helped to guide him in." Typical thoughts of some men!

Abuse also happens to driving instructors when the DVSA introduced the reverse and forward bay parking into the test. Usually, the public would not think twice about saying anything if it was an ordinary car reverse bay parking next to them in the car park. But, again, they think the instructor will let the learner damage their car. Really! We were preparing to do a reverse bay park, but another vehicle took up the space. The driver could see what we were trying to do, but no, she had to park there, even though other spaces were available. Now, I must have been in a bad mood and left a note on her car windscreen saying how rude she was. I found out a few days later she was an examiner's girlfriend. Oh, dear! However, nothing came of it, except hopefully, she would think twice next time. Maybe she did not tell him my views, or he was too embarrassed to say anything to me.

I heard another funny story on the radio about a woman in her 4 x 4, getting ready to reverse into a parking space in a multi-storey car park. A cocky lad drove forward into the space, came up to her, and said,

"That's what you can do if you can drive."

She retaliated by reversing into his car and squashing it against the wall.

She then said to him, "That's what you can do if you're filthy rich," and drove off. Nice one.

However, I did not hear or have much trouble with forward bay parking. It may be because people need to decipher what is happening sooner!

Another manoeuvre is the 'pull up on the right-hand side of the road, reverse for two car lengths and rejoin the traffic'. It can be scary when you first practice it, and some drivers give you a 'what the hell are you doing' look. Although it is not common practice to park on the right-hand side of the road (by the way, you should not park on the right-hand side of the road at night, except in a one-way street), the DVSA introduced it into the driving test because there are real-life situations when you may have to in daylight. Eventually, you get used to it.

In addition, included in the test is the controlled stop (emergency stop). It used to be in every test, but now it is one in every three. The examiner will explain how he will ask you to stop, and it is usually carried out in a 30 mph limit zone. The examiner will ensure it is safe before signalling to stop the car. After the stop, the examiner may say,

"Thank you. I will not be asking you to do that exercise again. Drive on when you are ready."

However, in an actual emergency, you must act accordingly.

Most pupils pick up the stop reasonably quickly. However, occasions have occurred when I have had to spend an hour's lesson, and more, with some pupils because they are too scared to do it, or their co-ordination hampers them. The procedure is to 'brake – clutch'. Do it as you say it, almost simultaneously pressing down the pedals.

Still, some people put their foot on the accelerator instead of the brake with the clutch down or press the clutch first, then the footbrake. After they have stopped, some become transfixed and cannot take their feet off the pedals or their hands off the steering wheel. Some of my girls have let go of the steering wheel to cover their faces, and others have screamed or shouted, "Noooooo," as they were doing it! Other pupils grip the steering wheel or at arm's length and/or have their faces distorted! Eventually, they relax and realise you only have to say to yourself, 'brake – clutch'. Probably it is because of waiting for the instruction, whereas in actual situations, it will be instinctive.

The reverse corner and the turn-in-the-road manoeuvres (no longer in the driving test) could also cause problems with the public. For example, one of my colleague's pupils was practising the reverse corner manoeuvre when a man came out of his house and knocked on the front passenger window. My colleague opened the window, and the man punched her in the face, swearing and shouting he had had enough of learners using his corner. She was shocked and called the police, who prosecuted him for assault.

I was teaching a friend of mine to drive. We were practising the reverse corner, where a bus stop was opposite the junction. Four people were sitting in the bus shelter, waiting for the bus. All fascinated by what was happening, as she was having trouble with the manoeuvre.

She finally succeeded and said,

"Well, I'm disappointed. I was expecting those onlookers to hold up scorecards giving me 10/10 or shouting out 'Oi'll give it foive' like Janice Nicholls did on the 1960s show Thank Your Lucky Stars, or was it Juke Box Jury? But, oh dear, I'm showing my age now," she said, laughing.

She had the same corner in her test, did it perfectly, and passed.

The turn-in-the-road was, I thought, the easiest manoeuvre to learn. However, some learners still needed help with it. Practising the manoeuvre with a lad took its toll on him and me. I was under the doctor for high blood pressure and was wearing a monitor. Cars started queueing on either side as we sat in the middle of the road with the lad, trying to get the reverse gear. After a while, the waiting cars decided they had had enough. They started hooting their horns and even driving past us, going up onto the pavement. I had to be patient with him to keep him calm whilst the impatient drivers were doing their stuff.

"What's the (swearing) matter with them? Can't they see I'm doing (swearing again) my best!" he exclaimed, with more swear words, being unprintable!

"Calm down, let them clear off, and we'll finish the manoeuvre," I said, trying to reassure him.

When I went to my doctor to see my results, I asked how my blood pressure was on the day and time of this manoeuvre. She looked at me and said,

"Wow, sky-high. What on earth was happening?"

Then, after explaining the situation to her, she laughed and said she remembered the manoeuvre during her driving lessons and had not found it easy.

For more information about manoeuvres and other procedures, go to GOV.UK Driving test: cars.

CHAPTER NINE

INCIDENTS AT THE TEST CENTRE

AN ANECDOTE FROM A COLLEAGUE'S PUPIL…

When the examiner asked my pupil to get in the car and make himself comfortable, he went and sat in the passenger seat!

Now imagine this! While waiting for my pupil's name to be called for her test, we heard feet stomping and muttering noises from somebody coming up the stairs. Then a lady burst into the waiting room in a frenzy and, in a broad Irish accent, asked,

"Is this the test waiting room, and is my friend too late for her test?" Nobody answered her, as the examiners were already coming into the waiting room and calling the candidates.

She was on her mobile, frantically shouting to her friend, saying she'd better get here quick, as an examiner had already called her name. We could hear her friend saying she'd only just found the toilet in the high street because the supermarket would not let her use theirs. Then, as the Irish woman explained to the examiner that her friend was looking for a toilet, the candidate rushed into the room. The examiner asked her name, but she went on saying in broad Irish,

"I was looking for a toilet. You know how it is. I've got a gippy stomach and thought I would poo myself."

"I don't wish to know that," he said. "I'll ask you again, is this your name ………?"

The candidate's friend said, "Yes, that's her name, so it is."

"Will you please be quiet! I'm asking the candidate, not you," he said. "Don't interrupt!"

Turning to the candidate, he said, "I take it you don't have an instructor?"

"Oh, no, sir. Do I need one?" she asked anxiously.

"No, it's not required," he replied.

Still interrupting, her friend said, "Oh, yes, that's right. I told her she didn't need one."

The examiner glared at the friend.

"Have you got a passenger mirror in the car?" he asked.

"No, she hasn't got one," her friend said.

"Will you please be quiet, madam? I've asked you to stop interfering. This is not your test," the examiner said, trying to keep his temper.

"Do you need one then, sir? I didn't think about that," said the candidate.

This meant he had to get the spare mirror from the examiner's office.

"Can I see your provisional licence, please?" he asked.

"Oh, no, sir, I've left it in the car," she replied.

So, with looks that could kill and showing his frustration, the examiner said,

"I'll have to see your licence when we get to the car. So lead the way to your vehicle when you're ready."

Suddenly, as the examiner and candidate were about to go down the stairs, the friend charged out of the waiting room, shouting,

"Ohhhh, let me get by you," (also invoking the Holy Family of J, M and J). "I've got to get the baby out of the car. We forgot the baby is in the car! What eejits, so we are!"

With that, she pushed through, rushing to get to the car.

I was sitting in the test waiting room with a colleague, watching this comedy act being played out. My colleague said,

"We have got to get down to the car park to see how this will pan out."

Sure enough, a girl aged about eleven got out of the car with the baby in her arms. Also, the woman taking her test was driving a 4 x 4 and had parked in the wrong car park. The examiner, being disabled, could not walk fast, so as he had to walk further to the car, it also took up valuable time.

Finally, we saw him check her provisional licence, get into the car and leave the car park. Unfortunately, all the faffing about made it too late for us to stay when our pupils returned, so we never knew the outcome. This and the following story were the most hilarious incidents I have witnessed in the test centre waiting room. They could have been in a '*Carry On*' film.

It was 1st April (April Fools' Day), and Hazel, my pupil, and I were the only ones in the waiting room. Her examiner came in, followed by another examiner trying to guide him. Hazel's examiner was wearing black-rimmed glasses with thick glass lenses and was fumbling about, asking where she was, and looking for her in the opposite direction to where she was standing. It was farcical.

"Can I see your provisional licence, please," he said with a straight face, holding his hand out into thin air. So Hazel had to go in front of him to give him her licence. He took it and held it close-up to his glasses to read it.

Hazel looked at me, confused, but all she could see was me laughing!

"Lead the way to your vehicle. Do you mind if I put my hand on your shoulder so you can guide me?" the examiner asked.

"I suppose so," she said in bewilderment.

Again, she looked at me, but I was not very helpful, as I was still laughing. I followed them, and before they got to the stairs, the examiner came clean with her, and then she started laughing. This probably settled her nerves because she passed her test the first time.

When pupils did not show up for their test or the examiner was otherwise free, sometimes they would come into the waiting room to chat with the instructors. My pupil was out on her test, and she was the only candidate, so I was alone. The examiner told me a story of working in a London test centre where there had been many fraudulent tests, and a man had jumped through the glass of a first-floor window. The examiners at this centre realised they had often seen this man without an instructor. So, his examiner took time checking his details while another examiner rang the police. Now you would think the police would arrive quietly to catch him, but no, the sirens were blaring out, and the candidate heard them. That is when he jumped through the window. Blood was on the broken glass from cutting his leg, but he limped away before the police arrived at the test centre. He did not show up at that test centre again.

FACT – If someone impersonates another driver for a practical driving test, the theory test, or both. They and the driver being impersonated can face criminal prosecution, possibly resulting in a prison sentence.

One of my ladies, who was about to take her test, asked if she could dab some essential oils on her wrists to help calm her down, unlike the previous lady I mentioned. I said it was alright, and at least she asked. She got it out of her bag and dabbed it onto her wrists, and I had a sniff. However, while she was out on her test, I started having a little difficulty breathing, and my throat felt weird. But I felt better when she returned from the test. Unfortunately, she did not pass, so she booked another test and again asked if she could use the oils.

I said, "OK, but don't come near me cos of what happened last time."

"Oh, yeah, I forgot about that," she replied. "It should be OK. I'm only dabbing it on my wrists."

But, while she was out on her test, my breathing once again became difficult. My throat was closing in, and I came out in a rash. Panicking, I quickly went to the chemist a few doors from the centre. The pharmacist gave me some antihistamines and cream for the rash, which did the trick, and said I must be allergic to the oils. This time she passed, and I told her what had happened to me.

"Can you wrap the bottle of oils up so I can have an allergy test?" I asked.

"Yes, of course," she replied, wrapping it in a polythene bag she fortunately had.

I made an appointment with the local wholefood shop, which did allergy testing. But unfortunately, the allergist could not tell me what I was allergic to because the bottle contained different synthetic oils. Being synthetic was probably the problem. So, after those two incidents and the one in the *'Now the Real Thing'* chapter, I did not allow oils of any kind to be used again!

You can feel like a right half-wit if you fall over in the street. But when it happens walking through the car park towards the test office with your pupil, it is even more embarrassing. Bang, down I went, falling flat on my face!

"You OK?" Emma, my pupil, asked.

"Yeah, just feel a bit of a wally," I said as I rubbed my grazed hand and knee.

Emma's examiner saw me injured. "Are you alright?" he asked. "Do you want a drink of water?"

"No, thank you," I replied. "I'm OK, a bit shaken up, but no worries."

Emma wanted me to accompany her on the test, but the instructor must refrain from interfering. So I sat in the back, still dazed and not thinking correctly. When the examiner asked Emma to drive on, she checked around her before moving away; the trouble was, so was I! There I was, sitting bolt upright in my seat, looking around me as though I was hinting at what she should do!

"Mrs Carey," said the examiner. "Stop looking around. If you carry on, I shall have to abandon the test!"

"Er, sorry," I said. "I think I'm still in shock from falling over. I wasn't trying to assist Emma. Sorry."

The test went ahead, and she passed. However, after it had finished, the examiner said, "A word, please, Mrs Carey!"

I was a newcomer to the test centre and had to convince the examiner I was not interfering. So when we got out of the car, I got in first with my explanation.

"I'm sorry. I have no excuse other than I was still in shock from falling over," I explained.

"OK," said the examiner. "I'll accept your explanation, but don't let it happen again. If it does, I will stop the test!"

So, the lesson learnt from this scenario is not to fall over before a pupil's driving test!

Nowadays, examiners are trained in political correctness and should treat candidates with respect, as candidates should them. 99% of examiners are genuinely nice people. However, as in all walks of life, there is always one. If there is a rogue examiner and a candidate complains, the DVSA takes it seriously.

Indeed, there was a good working relationship between instructors and examiners at the test centres I used. However, years ago, I remember an examiner who could act coarsely and worked at a centre I often frequented. He was just on his markings, and I did not have any truck with him on how he tested my pupils because I knew it was their weakest point when he failed them.

Sadly, however, his attitude after passing someone was strange. If he failed them, he would be kind, telling them where they had gone wrong and hoping to see them again soon. However, if he passed anyone, he would not let them have their moment of happiness. Some girls/women would cry, and the boys/men would want revenge on him.

One lad I taught was so calm and laid back that nothing fazed him until he had his test with this examiner! It was when instructors could not listen in on the debrief the examiners would give the candidate. Still, I could see something was wrong by looking at my lad's red face. When the examiner got out of the car, he made a snide remark to me about how he nearly fell asleep because the boy was driving too slowly around the course. I did not understand this because they had arrived back at the test centre at the usual time.

When I got to the car, my lad said, "Oh, he made me so angry! He went on and on about how I drove too slowly. Look at my marking sheet. I've only got two faults. OK, one was for not making progress, but he wouldn't let up about it."

"Yes," I said. "I could see by the look on your red face you were getting annoyed. The good thing is you passed. The examiner wouldn't have passed you if you had been that bad. Try to forget what he said and enjoy that you've now got your licence."

He gradually calmed down on the way home, but his anger must have flared up again when he got indoors. I was also teaching his mum to drive, and I asked her how he was when he came home.

She laughed and said, "Oh, he was in such a mood, but his dad walked him to the pub for a celebratory drink. Just one thing, though, I hope I don't get this examiner for my test!" Luckily, she didn't.

On another occasion, I had a pupil, Isla, who had moved down from Scotland, and on checking her licence (then a paper licence), found it still had her old address. I told her she needed to exchange it for showing her new address as she was now permanently living here in England and must remember to sign the new licence. So, in the following six or seven lessons, I asked Isla if she had got the new one and had signed it, and each time she said no. Then, as you do, I forgot to ask her again.

At that time, if a candidate's licence was not signed, the examiner would ask them to sign it in front of them. However, a new rule was if a candidate's licence was unsigned, the examiner could not take them for their test. However, as it was a new rule, they were lenient, asking the candidate to sign the licence before going out on their test. We arrived at the test centre, and this examiner called her name. She went over to him, and he asked to see her licence. Unbeknown to me, she had changed it but had yet to sign it. He then asked who her instructor was; of course, it was me!

He looked at me and unpleasantly said, "I might have known it was her!"

She tried to explain what had happened and apologised, but he was not listening. Instead, he got her to sign the licence and moaned as they went to the car. Regrettably, because it was a hectic time of the year, we had to park in another car park, and he was also unhappy about that.

When they left the waiting room, the other instructors asked if I would let him get away with how he spoke to me. No way was I going to, and I reported him to the Test Manager, explaining what had happened and how he had treated my pupil. He then asked if I wanted to have him apologise to me, and he would make sure he did. But an apology never came, only him blanking me for the following three months when finally, I got "Good morning" from him. However, I did worry during this time about how he would treat my future pupils, but he carried on in his usual way.

For some reason, this examiner was transferred to another test centre for about a year. Hence, his reputation died down but soon flared up when he returned. My daughter had him for her second test. She passed, and he was not rude to her and made no jibe to me about her driving. Perhaps he thought it was best not to. On her first test, she had the examiner who had passed my son the first time. When the examiners came into the waiting room, her examiner called her using names such as Miss Fairy and Miss Canary, other than her real name. She was getting uptight and could not see its funny side because she was so nervous. He tried to settle her nerves, but it backfired, and she did not pass. He apologised to me for failing her, but she made a mistake, and examiners cannot discriminate. I told him not to worry and thanked him for trying to calm her nerves. Thankfully, she got her second test within a few weeks and passed. It was the first test of the day, and luckily, the preceding day, when they changed from asking questions at the end of the test to sitting the theory test.

It is a criminal offence to bribe examiners in the UK. You could try, but they will rebuke you immediately. If there is a dishonest examiner, they are taking the risk of being caught. If caught, they will suffer grave consequences, and so will you.

One of my girls, a foreigner to this country, asked me about bribing the examiner, as her homeland was known for it. I, of course, said an emphatic "NO." On her test day, we ran late and rushed into the test centre. Her examiner was waiting for her, and we apologised for being late. Five minutes are acceptable, but examiners can cancel the test if you are not there at the allotted time. Unfortunately, she had put money in her driving licence wallet, unbeknown to me. As the examiner took the wallet and saw the money, he immediately dropped it onto the floor.

He exclaimed, "We do not take bribes here!" Quickly thinking, I said, "Oh, hell. I didn't know she had put *my* money in the wallet." Then bent down to pick it up. As a regular instructor at this test centre, he knew and believed me. It could have been a different story if I had been at another test centre where I was unknown. I questioned her about it after her test (she passed), but she was adamant she was not trying to bribe him. The jury is out on that one!

There were no designated parking bays for test candidates at one of the test centres. After returning from a test, the candidate would have to stop in the aisle. Sometimes, people would return to their cars simultaneously, wanting to move out of the parking bay. On one occasion, this happened, and the examiner asked the candidate to move ahead a little more so the person could move out. Unfortunately, the candidate shot forward so much that she knocked down an examiner's motorbike. Needless to say, she did not pass. How unfortunate! Have to say this was not one of my pupils.

While sitting in the waiting room with another instructor, a foreign gentleman came in and said he was late for his test. We told him to knock on the examiner's door, but the test would probably not go ahead because he was too late. The examiner opened the door, told the man he was too late, and explained why. The man pleaded with the examiner to take him out, saying he would pay him for doing so and did not care if he failed as long as he could take the test. Of course, the examiner refused and shut the door on him. The man went away, but ten minutes later returned, banging on the examiner's door, using abusive language, calling him a racist and threatening to kill him. My colleague and I intervened, but the man was becoming violent. Then luckily, a senior examiner visiting the test centre came along. So, as the four of us were standing around him, he gave up and went away. If the examiner had been alone, goodness knows what could have happened.

I would think ahead for when I knew my pupils would be ready for their driving test and leave it up to them to book a date. One of my lads, Martin, told me his mum had booked his test, and he gave me the date and time, which I wrote in my diary. The day before his test, we were in the test car park at the same time as his test would be the following day. We watched the examiners go through the procedures with the candidates and then drive off.

"That'll be you tomorrow," I said.

"Yeah, a bit nerve-racking watching them, but I'll be OK," he replied.

"You've just got to go for it. You'll be fine," I said, trying to encourage him.

"It's alright for you. You're not the one doing it!" Martin exclaimed.

"I can assure you I've had to suffer loads of tests in my lifetime," I answered.

We arrived at the test centre the next day, but there appeared to be too many candidates waiting for their tests. Martin's name was not called, so an examiner went to check and told him his test had been the day before! The time when we were watching the candidates go out on their tests. When his mum was told, she was insistent she had booked the test for that day and even came to my house to check it with me on the booking site. Yes, she had told us the wrong date and had to concede it was her mistake. I felt sorry for Martin, but he did not have to wait too long for another date and thankfully passed the first time.

One time at a test centre, there were two BSM instructors. The examiners came in and called the candidates over to them. They went through the usual questions, then asked them to lead the way to their vehicles. We watched as our pupils and the two BSM candidates went to their cars, but the trouble was that each one went to the other one's car. Their instructors shouted, "No, no, no," and rushed to them. Still, the pupils and examiners were seated and belted up in the wrong car! After the instructors sorted it out, they returned to the test centre waiting room. The air was blue!

CHAPTER TEN

THE DRIVING TEST – THEORY AND PRACTICAL

ANECDOTES FROM COLLEAGUES' PUPILS...

Taking their theory tests, two pupils had a sign for a Ford. They thought it was for Ford cars. Both asked why they have signs for Ford cars but not others.

FACT – Voluntary driving tests, enacted in England in 1935, cost seven shillings and sixpence (37.5p), and the pass rate was 63%. The first person to pass was Mr Beere. There were no driving test centres, so the examiners would meet candidates at a designated spot, maybe a railway or bus station. It was on 1st June 1935 when a compulsory driving test came into effect and backdated to all drivers who started driving on or after 1st April 1934.

For many years you took only the practical test with rules of the road questions from the Highway Code being asked at the end of the test, usually only three or four questions. However, this finished when on the 1st July

1996, multiple-choice theory test questions, still based on the rules of the road, were implemented and passed before taking the practical test.

When the DVSA introduced the multiple-choice theory test, they advised driving instructors to teach theory lessons separately from driving. So, with another instructor, we hired a hall to give theory lessons with ten of his students and ten of mine attending. It went down well, with all the students passing for the first time.

Then, only 35 questions had to be answered, and the pass mark was 26 out of 35. However, on the 1st of October 1996, they raised the theory test pass mark from 26 out of 35 to 30 out of 35. Subsequently, the DVSA created a theory book containing questions and answers, killing the classroom lessons and allowing students to learn independently. Some people can study on their own and be capable of understanding the theory. However, others can find studying difficult, so I gave one-to-one lessons and was happy they passed with my help. On the 14th November 2002, the hazard perception test (pass mark 44 out of 75) was introduced to be taken after the multiple-choice theory questions. Both tests have to be passed together. The theory test pass mark was again changed on the 3rd September 2007 to 43 out of 50 questions. Then, on the 28th September 2020, they altered the layout of the theory test.

You can start practical lessons before you take the theory test/hazard perception test. It is good to do so, as it can help you understand the theory questions asked and gain knowledge of hazard perception. However, once you have passed the theory test/hazard perception test, there is a time limit of two years for you to take the practical test. You can find more information on GOV.UK/Take a practice theory test/hazard perception test. Once passed the practical test is within your reach.

Unfortunately, rumours go around about examiners. You will find some people spread stories because they have failed the test. They need to find an excuse. They think it is not their fault because it is Monday, and the examiners are in a mood for having to come back to work. Take the test at the beginning of the month because they already have their quota by the end. Do not take your test on a Friday because the examiners can only pass ten weekly tests. Or the examiner did not explain things to me clearly, or they did not like me because of how I dressed, my piercings, and so on. Or they blame their driving instructor!

Examiners do not/should not deliberately fail you. They have a job to do, which is to make sure you are a safe driver. You are not there for them; you are there for yourself because passing your driving test will give you freedom. So you must show the examiner you are a safe driver and worthy of being let loose on the road.

You are tested on the following categories
For more information, see Gov.UK – Driving test: cars

Eyesight test	Three chances to prove your vision is acceptable.
Controlled stop	Stopping the car quickly and maintaining control of the vehicle.
Reversing manoeuvres	Four manoeuvres. Only one is tested.
Vehicle checks	Examiners will ask one tell question at the beginning of the test/one show question while driving.
Precautions	Adjust the seat and mirrors correctly/and able to operate all controls safely.
Control	Operating all controls competently/hand positioning and holding the steering wheel correctly.
Move off	Safely and in control.
Use of mirrors	Effective use of mirrors when signalling/changing direction/changing speed.
Signals	Give signals correctly/necessary/in good time.
Clearance/obstructions	Give adequate clearance to parked vehicles/other obstructions.
Response to signs/signals	Act on traffic signs/lights/road markings/traffic controllers/other road users.
Use of speed	Obeying speed limits/driving to the conditions of the road.

Safe following distance	Keeping to the two-second rule when driving/seeing tyres and tarmac of the lead vehicle when queuing.
Progress	Driving too slow for the road conditions/being over cautious.
Junctions	Approach speed/observation/position correctly/turning safely.
Judgement	When overtaking/meeting other traffic/crossing the path of other vehicles.
Positioning	When normally driving/proper lane discipline/avoiding kerbs.
Pedestrian crossings	Giving priority to pedestrians/approach speed/complying with traffic lights.
Position/normal stops	Making normal stops in a safe/legal/convenient position.
Awareness/Planning	Judgement of other road users/acting in good time.
Ancillary controls	Use of windscreen wipers/demisters/air conditioning.
Pass or Fail?	Good luck!

You used to have a marking sheet given to you, but nowadays, examiners use a tablet and send your copy to you via email.

If you have a 'driving fault', it is classed as something not potentially dangerous. You are allowed up to fifteen of these faults. Sixteen is a fail! Still, if you keep repeating the same driving fault, it could become a 'serious fault', and just one serious fault means you will fail the test. This is because of potential danger being caused to others or risks to yourself. If the examiner thinks you are a real danger on the road, they will stop the test for public safety. Examiners cannot drive the instructor's car, so they will walk back to the test centre. They will ask if you would like to walk with them or wait in the car for your instructor.

Show Me/Tell Me questions were introduced on the 4th December 2017. The Tell Me question will be asked at the beginning of your practical test. The Show Me part will be asked as you drive. One examiner, in the same week, asked two of my pupils a tell question about the tyres. Instead of saying 'the entire outer circumference of the tyre', they both said 'circumstance'! The examiner smiled broadly after the second pupil had used the same word. As the test progresses, there will be 20 minutes of independent driving. Either direction from a sat nav or following traffic signs.

So why do people fail the practical test? Maybe they are not ready or are ready, but nerves get such a hold on them they cannot cope with the pressure and make silly mistakes. I would tell my pupils I wanted them to be above the average test standards so they could be 90% sure of passing, and the odd 10% would fall to the luck of the day and the nerves. It is the examiner's job to make sure (and yours to prove to them, as I have already stated) that you are good enough to pass the test and be safe on the road.

It is not only the mechanical side of learning to drive a car but also perceptiveness (that is why you take a hazard perception test to help you understand perception). It is a mad world on the road, so you must gain a sixth sense, knowing what will happen before it does. This takes time, and you will only have that full ability after passing your test once you have been on the road for a while.

The DVSA recommends forty-four hours of professional tuition and twenty-two hours of private practice (at the time of writing). Of course, this depends on the learner's ability, who may need more or less. Some people think they are ready for their practical test when they are not, especially when they pass the theory test with flying colours. They then want to book the practical. But, even though they have passed the theory, most people still need more practice to be ready to take the practical test. They also go too strongly with the DVSA's recommendation, as written above, which they feel is all they need. Even if you give that person a mock test and they fail miserably, they do not understand that they need more time to be ready and think you are just taking their money. For instance, I had two girls who began learning one January. One girl was prepared for her test in September and passed the first time, but the other girl was not ready for hers until the following March and failed it on road positioning. She passed on her second attempt in May.

Unfortunately, some parents with bright sons or daughters think they will take to driving instantly. Therefore, they will not listen to the advice of their instructor. It is hard to understand their reasoning; fortunately, I have had only a few cases. I remember one girl who passed her theory and wanted to book her driving test. I told her she was not ready and would not be until another five months (based on a two-hour weekly lesson). However, her parents thought she was prepared for her test because she had had the DVSA's recommended amount of lessons and private practice. So the father texted me to say, in his opinion, his daughter was ready and would not need my services any longer. I texted him back, explaining she had failed her mock test on the following items. One was entering a busy dual carriageway from an acceleration lane. She went into panic mode and wanted to pull out in front of a lorry, which would have caused a serious accident and possibly killed her if she had been alone. Also, there were other serious driver faults. I suggested he attend a driving lesson to see her progress, but he declined and thought he knew best.

Also, the parent of a lad I was teaching decided he was ready for his test. Again, I explained it would be at least another four months for him to be prepared. I saw the parent four or five months after he had left me and was told he had *just* passed his test. So I was right!

As a colleague said, "It's good to see 'L' plates still on the learner driver's private car or learning with another instructor months after they have left you."

Another thing that amazes me is why new drivers feel they can drive high-powered cars when they may have been learning in a moderate-engine car. It is an accident waiting to happen. Do they not realise the danger? They need more experience driving independently and dealing with the real world before upping the engine size.

When you teach people from other countries where the test is less stringent than ours, instilling in them that the UK test is a gruelling test is frustrating for them, but they have to come to terms with it and be ready. I have taught various nationalities, and many think they only want a few lessons to be done and dusted and are shocked when they realise how much they have to learn to pass our test.

For instance, I taught two Polish sisters to drive. One picked it up early, but the other found it difficult. She was getting agitated about me not entering her for her driving test, as her sister had hers booked. She said she would return to Poland to take her test and have a driving licence. I told her to go ahead, but she could kill herself and others when she returned and drove here. We had a long chat about it, and luckily she believed what I had said. It took another six months before she was ready for her first test, which she failed on one serious and a couple of driver faults. Passing on her second test, she told me she was glad I had said about killing herself because I was right, and now she realised how good she had to be to pass the test and be safe on the road.

Many learner drivers do not want others to know when their practical driving test is. Still, they do usually tell their parents and maybe their family. However, one of my girls did not want anyone to know, not even her parents. The only people who knew were herself, her boss because she needed time off work, and me. So we devised a plan for how I could pick her up from her house without her parents being suspicious. She left for work as usual but waited in a café near where she lived. Then went back home after her parents had gone to work and waited for me to come and pick her up. The plan worked, and she passed the first time.

Two girls bugged me about their learning and passing. In every lesson, I would get an arm's length of explanation on why they will never be a driver, what they would fail on, and should I honestly book my test, as you know, I would fail. Finally, they booked their tests, but it got even more unbearable to listen to them, and when the day came for their test, the first thing they said when they got in the car was,

"You know I'm going to fail!"

They both wanted me to go with them on the test for moral support and as I watched them go around the course, I knew they would pass. Both were ecstatic and overdoing the thanking and trying to kiss the examiner when told they had passed. Then, on the way home declared they had enjoyed the test! What! After all the grief they had given me in lessons, I could not believe they were saying this to me.

The following stories are about what can happen on a driving test.

Your examiner is now your passenger, and you are taking them for a ride in your car. They cannot instruct you because you will be alone when driving after you pass. You need to be more competent if they have to intervene, verbally or in action.

One of my girls failed her test three times on the same road positioning fault. I could not understand why, and I was nitpicking with her road positioning in lessons, but everything was fine. So on her fourth test, I said I wanted to go out with her. She was getting on OK until we came to a roundabout, and she exited onto a dual carriageway unnecessarily into the right-hand lane. The examiner was trying by his body language to get her to move back to the left-hand lane. Still, she was not noticing him and only when he asked her to turn left at the next roundabout did she go into the left-hand lane. By the way, I had a dad tell his son that only women went into the left-hand lane when exiting a roundabout! I soon put him right. Is there a pun there? She probably would have been fine if she had quickly taken up the left-hand lane. So, of course, she failed the test for road positioning yet again. I had to take her to where it happened, and she told me she had exited the roundabouts into the right-hand lane on all three previous tests. No wonder I could not understand why she kept failing in road positioning, as she had not been doing that in her driving lessons. So on her fifth test, she passed! She got fed up with failing and her friends pestering her. I told her to tell them she had packed it in and put a different name for her in my book. However, I was simultaneously teaching her best friend, and she tried to trick me into telling her she still was having lessons.

One day, she said to me, "I like the colour of Lacy's hair. Don't you?"

I nearly fell into the trap but replied, "How do I know? I haven't seen her."

"Ha-ha, there're no flies on you! I know she's still learning," she said, looking at me for a reaction.

"Well, I think you'll find she isn't," I said.

She looked at me with disbelief on her face.

One pupil can go around a test route and have it as easy as anything, while another can go the same way, and everything happens. It is the luck of the draw. One of my girls had an incident on the first roundabout she came to on the test. She was clear from the right and moved into the roundabout but realised the car from her left would not stop and give way to her. So she made an emergency stop in the middle of the roundabout. The examiner asked her if she was alright and said to drive on when she was ready. He also put his clipboard with the marking sheet on the floor, so she thought, that's it, I have failed, but carried on driving as best she could. When they got back to the centre, to her surprise, the examiner said,

"I am very pleased to say you have passed, and thank you for saving my life."

"What!" she exclaimed. "I thought I'd failed because of what happened at the roundabout and saw you put your board on the floor."

"No," he said. "You drove well and handled the situation excellently. You should feel very proud of yourself."

On another occasion on the same route, a pupil took the first roundabout to the right, left at the end of the road, and approached a bridge controlled by traffic lights. They were on green. So, she went to cross over the bridge only to be faced by an oncoming lorry, which had jumped a red light on the other side. She quickly pulled the car over to the left, enabling her to get into a space there, and the lorry sped through. She got herself together and then went over the bridge, where a dumper truck was pulling out in front of her from a building site. So an emergency stop was called for. However, she continued driving and was directed onto a dual carriageway approaching a large roundabout. A major accident had happened, and police were directing traffic through. She handled the situation and finally returned to the centre without more trouble. To her surprise, she passed, and the examiner said she needed a stiff drink after what she had been through.

Another one of my girls unwittingly took the wrong direction five times but still passed her test. Unfortunately, when the examiner asked her to take another turn, she went wrong again. However, this time she realised.

"Oh," she said. "You asked me to turn left, and I've gone right, sorry."

"Yes, you have, but don't worry, you've already taken the wrong direction four times!" the examiner calmly said.

"Oh no, I'm so sorry. I didn't mean to," she replied.

"Just carry on with your driving and concentrate," he answered.

So taking the wrong direction does not fail you if you have done it correctly. The moral to these stories is if you show you are in control, have awareness about yourself and act accordingly, when something like the above happens, the examiner will realise you can cope with difficult situations. However, if you turn into a 'no entry road' or take, heaven forbid, the wrong entry onto a dual carriageway facing oncoming traffic, you will definitely fail. One of my colleagues had a pupil take the wrong turn and landed on a motorway, so the test had to be terminated.

I have had many chatty pupils as they drove, with me throwing in instructions or interjecting because they made mistakes. Chloe, however, I do not know how I taught her to drive because she never stopped talking. She was a competent girl, picking driving up quickly. Finally, we decided she should apply for her driving test, and the day came.

"Chloe," I said.

"Yes," she answered.

"You know, when you're out with the examiner, can you just concentrate on driving and not talk so much, please?" I tentatively asked her.

"Oh, I know I talk a lot. It's just me, but I will try not to on my test," she replied.

"Good girl. I need you to concentrate," I said with concern.

"Don't worry," she replied.

She asked me to go with her on the test, and I sat in the back, enjoying the ride. She was quiet until the examiner began talking. That was it! It was verbal diarrhoea from then on, so much so the examiner had to tell her to concentrate after she took a wrong turn. However, she drove well and passed with just two driver faults.

"Well, I did it," she said proudly. "And, I chatted with the examiner, so there."

That put me in my place!

Then there were the cheeky lads who would make me laugh while I tried to explain, no, telling them off for what they had done wrong. From one lad who was the worst of them, I would get,

"I like your hair today, Brenda. That's a nice dress you have on. You're looking good today, Brenda."

"Look, I'm trying to teach you to drive properly," I would answer him, trying to keep a straight face.

"Stop trying to flatter me! Do you *want* to pass your driving test?" I asked.

Nevertheless, he continued with the flattery, but somehow I taught him to drive appropriately. However, I was concerned about how he would be with a female examiner when taking his practical test. But, he had a male examiner who I did not think would appreciate his sense of humour. So it was a catch-22 situation.

When he left for his test, I whispered,

"Behave yourself!"

However, when he finished the test, he passed with just four faults.

"How did you get on with him?" I asked.

"Oh, he was alright. We talked about football all the way around the route, and I had him laughing in the end!"

So, either he distracted the examiner with his banter, or he had listened to me and drove correctly. Hopefully, it was the latter!

I was teaching a lad who was an Oxford graduate and studied politics. In the lesson before his test, we entered a road where a large branch had fallen off a tree. He was heading straight for it without awareness.

"Mind the branch," I shouted, grabbing the steering wheel to swerve around it.

"Sorry, Brenda, I wasn't thinking," he said.

"Well, you'd better think. You've got your test in half an hour," I said, trying not to get any more uptight than I already was.

When he returned from his test, I walked over to listen to the debrief, and the look on his face said it all.

"You didn't, did you?" I asked, exactly knowing what had happened.

"If you mean he nearly hit a tree branch in the road, then yes, that's what happened," said the examiner.

I looked at him in disbelief and got, "Sorry, Brenda," from him.

On the way home, I started laughing and said,

"When you make Prime Minister in thirty-odd years, I will tell everyone how you failed your first driving test."

"Ha ha, very funny," he indignantly replied.

Years ago, the driving test included arm signals. One was to give a slowing down arm signal if you were the lead vehicle approaching a zebra crossing. This was to inform the pedestrians and other traffic you would stop at the crossing. Although phased out in 1975, one examiner at a test centre I frequented still preferred it done. The word on the street was that someone had knocked him down while on a zebra crossing, and he was seriously injured. Being you never knew who the examiner would be, I would ask my pupils to open the driver's window on entering the High Street and give the arm signal if they were the lead vehicle. I began teaching a foreign lady, and I explained about an examiner at this test centre where she would take her test who insisted on using the arm signal if she were the lead vehicle.

"Well," she said, "I think it's stupid, and I'm not doing it."

"If you don't," I replied. "You might fail because you think it's stupid."

However, she was adamant about it. Well, you can guess who she had, and unfortunately, she was the lead vehicle and had to stop at the crossing to let pedestrians cross. She did not signal, so it opened up to the examiner to ask a question about when approaching a zebra crossing. She told him it was stupid and they did not have to do it in her country. So, not being happy with the answer, he failed her. She might have passed if she had appeased him and explained the procedure. I was cross with her. What would happen if he were her examiner for her next test? As luck would have it, she did not get him or have to do the arm signal because the crossing was clear of pedestrians and passed.

I taught a close friend to drive. She had an examiner who, sometimes, was not good-humoured, and I was hoping she would not have him. Now my face must have dropped when he called her name. She turned to me and saw the look on my face. Then started asking what the problem was.

"What's the matter?" she asked.

"Nothing! Go on. He's called you again," I replied.

She kept looking at me as she walked over to him, and I gave a cheery smile, trying to encourage her. Luckily he was good-humoured, and as they walked towards the car, he asked her what she did for a living. She replied she was just a housewife with a baby. He said not to say that as housewives and mothers work hard. He had been off work for the last fortnight, apparently looking after his five foster children while his wife was in the hospital, and had learnt how hard the work was. She then told him taking her driving test was worse than having a baby, to which he quipped he had no gas and air in the car. When the driving had finished, he then asked the questions on the Highway Code, and one of them she did not quite know what he was getting at.

She said, "My mind has gone blank. Why don't you ask me a question about stopping distances? I know them all."

"No," the examiner replied. "I am asking you this question," and repeated it.

"I can't remember," she replied anxiously. "But I know all the stopping distances. Go on, ask me."

He grinned at her and said, "OK, you've passed."

She then said, "Why didn't you ask me the question differently? I might have known better what you were getting at."

"I think, Mrs Evans, we'd better leave it there. Don't you?" he replied.

Horrors of horrors. But hooray, she passed the first time, although she was cheeky. Later I taught her lovely daughter, who passed for the first time.

In one particular town, a mini-roundabout led into a small dual carriageway and practised in lessons. Still, one of my pupils oversteered and tried to go up the right-hand side of the carriageway on her driving test. The examiner had to stop the test and settle her in the safest position. However, he had to leave her crying because she did not want to walk back to the test centre with him. Thankfully, it happened up the road from the test centre. I could get to her quickly after the examiner explained the situation. The poor girl was so upset, and I had to console her, get her home, and explain what had happened to her mum. On her next test, approaching the same mini-roundabout from a different direction, she had someone pull out on her from the left, to which she did an emergency stop. She passed this time, and the examiner congratulated her on controlling the situation. He said she acted quickly on nearly being 'T-boned'.

Sadly, while another pupil was on her test, the prong part of a buckle from a horse's saddle girth had gone into a tyre. The examiner and my pupil did not know this had happened until a pedestrian knocked on the passenger's front window as they waited at a junction. The pedestrian told them he could see something sticking out from the tyre, and the examiner got out of the car to inspect it. Although the tyre was still up, the test had to be stopped, so they both walked back to the test centre. The examiner told her she only had to drive back to the test centre and, up to then, she had passed. She was gutted.

I had a lad who, let us say, was a quick driver. I was forever telling him to slow down, not only with his speed but also when exercising manoeuvres. He practised driving with his dad, who also told him off for being too fast. The day before his test, he had a lesson, and I nagged him about his speed. Then he drove with his dad in the evening, who also warned him. So, when I picked him up the next day for his test, he said not to worry as he would take it steadily. But, unfortunately, he went the opposite way and failed because he drove too slowly! That evening, I had a telephone call from his dad to say it was his fault for failing because he had really laid into him the evening before. I felt just as guilty doing the same thing, but it turned out alright in the end, as he passed on the second attempt with only one fault.

When practising the parallel park manoeuvre, a lad would bring the car in extremely close to the kerb but cleared it whenever he did the procedure. I said I did not like him coming in so close and worried it would go wrong on his test. He got the manoeuvre on the day, and the inevitable happened. Knowing he would hit the kerb, he pulled out to do it again. Now you only have limited time and attempts to carry out any manoeuvre, and time was running out. When they returned to the test centre car park, I walked over to the examiner, saw his face, and knowingly said he had failed and was in the parallel park.

"How do you know that?" was his answer.

I explained what happened during his driving lessons. The examiner asked me to look at his test sheet, and the only fault he had was the failure fault for the parallel park. He said he had allowed him extra time to do the manoeuvre because he had a clean sheet and did not want him to go down on it, and I thanked him. Understandably, the lad was in a terrible mood with himself on the way home; it was not a pleasant drive. However, he passed with a different examiner on his second attempt and had no faults.

Another lad I taught was in a critical situation on his first test. He had only been on the road for five minutes when it happened. He proceeded towards an obscure mini-roundabout, and as he looked to his right, he saw a car approaching the roundabout at speed with its left signal on. My lad moved onto the roundabout, but the other driver turned right instead, missing my car by inches. He was shocked, and the examiner asked if he wanted to continue his test, but he didn't. However, they had to drive further down the road before the examiner could park him safely and asked if he wanted to walk back to the test centre. My lad said no, and he would be alright. I had gone for a cup of coffee with another instructor. When we returned to the car park and the other tests were coming in, I was worried about where he was because it was getting late. Then the examiner appeared and told me what had happened. My lad had been waiting for me for just over an hour. I felt so sorry for him. We discussed what had happened as I drove him home, hoping it would not put him off driving. It did not, but he said he had learnt his lesson on observation and should have realised what kind of driver the other one was. He passed the following test with just one fault and was a better driver through the incident.

A colleague of mine had a girl fail on steering. She could not understand why she had failed, nor could her instructor. Then, the examiners did not give explanations at the end of the test. So the instructor sent off for a report. Apparently, she wore a ring which she had not worn when learning. As she was steering, the ring kept twisting, and she put her hands high on the steering wheel to correct its position. So a warning! It is not worth wearing something you have not worn before in case it distracts you. If you have not worn it before, do not wear it on the day!

It was the wasp time of the year. At a test centre I frequented, my pupil and I saw a motorbike rider on his test come into the car park. The rider jumped quickly off his bike, frantically getting his helmet off. Scarily, a wasp had got inside his helmet and stung his face.

Similarly, my pupil, Pat, was taking her test and had the driver's window open. A wasp flew into the car and buzzed around her and the examiner. He opened the passenger window and was trying to flick it out.

"Would you like me to park up?" Pat calmly asked.

"Er, yes, please," the examiner gratefully replied.

They got the wasp out of the car, and Pat continued her test, and she passed. The examiner congratulated her on keeping calm and controlling the situation.

Some people cry when they are happy. I had a lady who burst into tears when the examiner told her she had passed. She cried as we drove home and kept saying,

"I've passed! I've passed! Can you believe it? I've passed!"

"Yep, you have, and you'd better stop crying; otherwise, your husband will think you've failed," I said.

We arrived at her house, and her children and husband were looking out of the window. They saw us and came rushing out because they could see she was crying.

"Oh, I'm so sorry you've failed," her husband said and hugged her.

I laughed and said, "No, she hasn't; she's passed!"

He looked at her and said, "Why are you crying?"

"Because I'm happy," she replied.

So then she was laughing and crying at the same time! So, I left her still crying and her husband thanking me as he took her indoors.

Another one of my pupils failed on the mirrors. She wore glasses and said to the examiner that he probably did not see her eyes move when she looked in the mirror. The examiner's reply was,

"I see everything!"

All my pupils have been grateful to me for passing their tests and getting on the road. As I have said, it can be a complete life-changer because they are now independent. Can go for a job which was initially too far away for them to travel to. Visit family and friends more often or move house. Once you have had the first lesson, you may feel it is not impossible to learn to drive. Anything and everything is possible if you put your mind to it and genuinely want it.

I have had many 'Thank You' cards, chocolates, bottles of wine, flowers and potted plants, and a mug with 'Queen of Awesomeness' inscribed (which I still have). It has all been much appreciated on my part. Over my thirty-six years of teaching, I have taught 1,441 people to drive.

CHAPTER ELEVEN

DREAMS

AN ANECDOTE FROM ONE OF MY PUPILS…

"I had a horrible dream last night about a fox jumping into my car and eating me up. What do you reckon that was about?" he asked. "Probably, he's getting his own back on drivers running his mates over," I said.

A close friend, mentioned in a previous chapter, wanted to learn to drive but was quite nervous because she often dreamt about having an accident at a junction. So, when I became an instructor, her husband and I convinced her to learn. One day, we were out on a lesson in a quiet estate and coming towards an end-of-road. But unfortunately, she was not slowing down soon enough.

"Liddia, slow down. Use the brake," I said, but she wasn't responding.

"The brake, Liddia," I urgently said, but there was still no response.

So, I used my dual-control footbrake, which came away from its fitting and fell to the floor!

"S-t-o-p," I shouted. That made Liddia brake! "Oh, hell, we'll have to stop the lesson, so I can sort this out with the garage. They've not fitted the dual controls properly."

"See," Liddia said. "I told you I'd have an accident at a junction. My dream has come true."

"Well, at least it was with me, and you've scuppered it now," I said, trying to reassure her.

"If you say so," she replied.

Luckily we were alright, and we started laughing, which settled our nerves. But unfortunately, I had to take over and drive her home before going to the garage to complain."

The car was new, and the garage had installed the dual controls. So their mechanic had a lot to answer for. I had already had occasions to complain to this garage about other issues (see *'Breakdowns'* chapter), and this was the last straw. Their slogan was 'Peace of Mind Part of the Deal'. So, I stormed in and made a scene, shouting,

"Peace of mind part of the deal? You have a long way to go!" and slammed the brake on the counter.

Customers and staff were staring at me. The manager quickly got me into his office, acting like I was making something out of nothing. I told him to stop patronising me and deal with the situation NOW. I said I wanted compensation for the lessons I had to cancel. So they offered to pay for petrol and gave me a receipt. I asked if I could use it twice because the amount on the receipt was more than I would pay for petrol in one go. They said no, only one receipt could be issued. So I sarcastically asked them to strap another petrol tank onto my tank, so I could use all the monies. So yes, I got two receipts but did not use the garage again.

Some dreams my pupils have had are hilarious. For example, a foster mother I taught dreamt she took her test in an old-fashioned coach pram. She was sitting in the pram, facing the handlebar, and it had the steering wheel attached to it. Behind her, under the hood, was her sister, acting as the examiner. The outcome was her sister said not in a thousand years would she pass her test. That did not give her confidence, but she passed her driving test on the second occasion. By the way, she was one of my pupils involved in an accident on the way to her first test. So despite the accident and the dream, she succeeded.

Another pupil's driving test was looming fast, but she had not got into the habit of checking her mirrors regularly. So I nagged her about it in her lesson the week before her test. When I picked her up for the test, she said,

"I had this horrible nightmare last night, and it's all your fault."

"How come?" I asked. "What did I do?"

"You nagged me so much about the mirrors. I dreamt all these mirrors surrounded my bed with eyes, legs and arms," she replied. It was terrifying! But she passed her test for the first time and had no mirror faults. So my nagging paid off.

An American lady I taught had been watching a cowboy film before going to bed one night. She dreamt the actor in the film was her examiner. He had a cowboy hat on, boots with spurs, and a gun belt with a gun in it. The year she took her test was about 1989, yet in her dream, he told her she would not pass her test until 1968. She had gone back 20-odd years in her dream, so what was that all about?

Another pupil dreamt he was taking his test driving along a beach. The examiner was in the front, and I was sitting in the back, and I suddenly shouted for my pupil to stop the car. He did, and I got out and walked into the sea. Plainly, he was driving so badly I wanted to drown myself!

Someone else dreamt they took their test in a 'Noddy' car with 'Big Ears' being their examiner. Another pupil dreamt of the examiner running alongside the car instead of being in the car.

How strange is the mind?

CHAPTER TWELVE

PETROL STATIONS

AN ANECDOTE FROM ONE OF MY PUPILS…

"I've been told I don't need to fill up with petrol straight away if I run out of it," he said. "Oh, yeah," I replied. "How will you move the car if you have no petrol?" "Well," he said. "I've been told the car will still run on the fumes in the tank for a while longer!"

You might think driving into a petrol station is just an everyday thing. Well, my experience is the unexpected can happen. While waiting behind a car about to be filled with petrol, a man took the hose out of the pump, placed the nozzle into the fuel filler inlet, and started pumping. As the petrol came into the hose, it disengaged itself from the nozzle. The poor man was panicking, with petrol flying everywhere, including him. Finally, the petrol attendant came running out of the station's shop, realised what was happening and ran back to turn the pump off. It only needed a spark to set the whole garage alight!

So I calmly told my pupil, "I think we should get out of here before there's an explosion and we say goodbye to the world!"

I heard nothing about it on the news, so presumably, everything got sorted!

On driving into a petrol station, a lad raced past us to get to the pump before we did. He showed off in front of his mates and thought he was being clever. However, he made himself look like an idiot as he nearly hit the first pump. Still, he caught and pulled out the three hoses attached to it and the three attached to the second pump, then came to a grinding halt just before hitting the station's shop. As you can imagine, the petrol attendant was furious and let his feelings known to the halfwit lad.

One winter, I had to get some petrol, and it had been snowing and freezing overnight. It was mid-morning, and the unsalted snow became compacted on the road. As a result, I was driving extremely slowly, and as I was about to drive into the petrol station, I lost control, and the car slid towards the pumps. I could only watch my car take me to my potential demise.

"Oh dear God, I am going to die. Goodbye, world," I cried, seeing my life flash before me. "I am going to be petrol-i-fried!" Get it? Luckily, the car stopped itself just as it reached the first pump; what a near miss!

Since the following incident, I have always ensured I had enough petrol in the tank. A lad was practising hill starts, and he kept stalling the car. I could not understand why, as he did all the right things.

"Er, John," I said. "I don't understand what's going on. You're normally good at hill starts."

"Yeah, I know, and it's getting on my frigging nerves!" he exclaimed.

Then I noticed the petrol gauge. It was showing empty!

"Er, I think I know the problem," I apprehensively said.

"What's the problem then?" he asked.

"No petrol in the tank!" I declared.

"You what? You're joking with me. I thought I was going mad because it wasn't working," he replied.

"Nope! I'm not joking! I'm now off to the petrol station with the petrol can to fill it up. See you in a bit!" I cheerfully said. Fortunately, the petrol station was not that far away. He could do hill starts brilliantly with petrol in the tank!

It was the time when petrol stations were changing over their pumps to show litres instead of gallons. I was filling up but not looking at how much I was spending and needing clarification on how many litres I was pumping in. I walked into the station's shop to pay but needed more money because of my confusion. The attendant remarked I was not the only one getting confused (that made me feel better). She took my name and address and said I could return later to pay the rest, which I did. Whew! Now I only look at how much money I want to spend.

I was very late for a lesson, but the petrol tank was nearly empty. So I rushed into the petrol station and filled it up, and I should have looked correctly at the amount of money or the number of the pump. So, I told the attendant what I thought the number was without looking to see the location of my car. While driving to my pupil's house, I realised I had given the attendant the wrong number for the pump. I paid more than I should have. I paid for somebody else's petrol! So that was their lucky day!

On another day of hurrying, I pulled up next to the petrol pump and used the option to pay by card for quickness. I had not done this before and was concerned about how to do it. I stood by the car, took the petrol hose from its holder and thought about what to do. "OK, put your card into the slot and type in the PIN." Then it said to take out the petrol hose. Whoops, I had already done that, so what was I supposed to do next? Just try it. I turned to the filler cap and saw I had forgotten to open it. Help! Now panicking, how did I open the filler cap? I have only done this a thousand times before! I put the hose back into its holder and remembered how to open the cap, but I also flipped the bonnet lever. When I returned to the pump, it asked me if I wanted a receipt.

Talking to myself, I said, "Er, no. You'll have to start again, dimwit!"

Finally, I filled the tank. It would have been quicker for me to have paid at the counter. Then, as I was driving on the dual carriageway, the wind flicked the bonnet; thankfully, the catch did not let it fly up. Unfortunately, I had forgotten to close the bonnet, so I had to pull over into a lay-by to close it. So my excuse is (and I am sticking to it) when you have a thousand things on your mind and hurrying, stuff like this happens.

I would get my pupils to fill the petrol tank when needed. Then, as they finished filling the tank, I said to be careful and shake the residue off before taking the nozzle out of the filler inlet. However, no, they are not, and I have had to jump back, but still had the petrol residue flung over me. So my perfume for the day was "Petroleum Eau-de-Toilette!"

Teaching one of my nieces to drive, I got her to fill up the tank by herself and pay for it whilst I waited in the car.

"You did very well there, Marie," I said. "Off you go when you're ready."

As she was driving, I looked in my mirror and saw she had not put the petrol cap back on, which was hanging on its wire.

"Er, did you put the petrol cap back on, Marie?" I asked.

"I think I did. Why?" she asked.

"Well, I can see it is dangling down and having a swinging time," I quipped.

"Oh, no!" she exclaimed. "I'll pull over and put it back on. Sorry. That will make me remember to finish the job."

"Yep! Never mind, we've all done it. No worries." I said, reassuring her.

I pulled into a petrol station, but the only available space was to use a pump on the opposite side of the car's petrol filler inlet. However, I was not close enough to the pump and had to stretch the pipe around the car to get to it, and the sun was in my eyes, so I could not correctly see how much petrol I was pumping in. It was taking ages, and I could see an amount of money on the face of the pump. I thought it said £30 odd pounds, but it was only £3 something when I went to pay. I could tell what the attendant was thinking by the smirk on her face as I explained my mistake. But there you go; it makes life interesting.

I felt sorry for an elderly lady who got the hose nozzle stuck in the filler inlet and would not budge. The attendants came out to help her, as did a couple of other drivers, but it was definitely stuck. So, when I went into the petrol station a couple of days later, I asked how they had got on. They had to call a mechanic who had to break the nozzle, careful it did not fall into the tank. It was the only way to resolve it.

I had a Mexican stand-off one time. I had driven into the petrol station via the Entry sign, but a car came in from the No Entry sign and stopped in front of me. After we had filled up, paid for the petrol and got into our cars, the man motioned for me to reverse, but I sat there shaking my head and stared at him. He kept motioning, but there was no way I would give in. He was getting irate, but with an 'I don't care' look on my face and shrugging my shoulders, he had to reverse. Then I realised why he wanted me to reverse. He could not do it and was all over the place. That'll teach him, and one up to me, I thought, and laughed to myself. Perhaps next time, he will come in via the proper entrance!

One evening, it was late when I had filled up and was leaving the petrol station. I could see, in my mirror, two men getting out of their car and going straight into the station's shop. I learnt later they were hold-up merchants and robbed the station. Glad I left the scene before that happened!

So there you have it. Even the tiny task of filling the car with petrol can have its moments!

CHAPTER THIRTEEN

ANIMALS

AN ANECDOTE FROM A COLLEAGUE'S PUPIL...

After seeing a sign for an animal, a pupil said, "This is not a safe place for horses, frogs or deer to cross. They should put a zebra crossing on the road for them to use."

Most drivers dread an animal running out before them, especially on rural roads. The national default speed limit for these roads is 60 mph. Still, you should always drive to the road conditions and constantly expect the unexpected. When drivers have swerved to miss an animal, sometimes they come off worse. It can be a fraction of a second to decide what to do. Also, you must report certain animals to the police and others to your local council if you are involved in an accident with them. For more information, go to GOV.UK – Report a dead or injured animal.

All drivers should realise horses, with their riders, have every right to be on the road. In addition, every driver should be aware there could be a horse (or other creatures) just around the bend, especially on rural roads. If you meet a horse with a rider, they are not there to annoy you but to get to a bridle path or stables, so be patient. Follow the new Highway Code rules for horses issued on 29th January 2022.

While on her horse, my daughter had a run-in with a famous racing driver who thought he was on a racing circuit. He drove past her far too quickly, and her horse reared up. He stopped to say sorry, but she was not best pleased with him and told him so. Hopefully, he realised what a fool he had been.

It can be tricky when lone horses are on the road. For example, horses had escaped from their stables during one particular lesson. They were happily munching on grass at the side of the road. Luckily, it was being dealt with when we arrived, so we waited until the stable staff took them off the road and back home.

So, when approaching a bend in rural areas, be aware of what might be around the corner. Normally you would expect a horse, but not always. In another lesson, it was an enormous pig. A police constable was there, and it was hilarious to see this lone officer trying to get the pig out of the road and not succeeding. Finally, he stopped it from running around, and we could get through. Likewise, we dealt with piglets in two other areas where they had escaped from a farm, poor things.

One of my pupils was driving to her test. She was going around 50 mph and talking about how horrible it would be if an animal ran out in front of her. Then, about five seconds later, a rabbit ran out. I grabbed the steering wheel to stop her from swerving.

"Go, go, go," I shouted. "Don't stop."

We would have caused a severe accident if she had stopped dead, and I would not be here to tell the story.

She went silent and then cried, saying, "I don't want to take my test any longer." Luckily, there was a side road I could take her onto.

"Come on," I said, "I know what happened wasn't nice, but you can still do this test."

"If I do, will you tell the examiner what happened, please?"

"Of course, I will," I said. "But, unfortunately, the examiner might not be sympathetic because you have to cope with things like this."

"Then I'm not doing it!" she emphatically replied.

After a while, she calmed down, and I talked her into going ahead with the test. I explained to the examiner what had happened, but he did not comment. She did not pass the test but carried on to pass the second one. Even if this happens on your driving test (as mentioned in the '*Unusual Situations*' chapter about the squirrel), you must show the examiner you can cope with anything untoward. After all, when you are driving, split-second decisions will have to be made, weighing up the pros and cons of what is occurring around you, so you must prove yourself. One more incident in a country lane concerning a rabbit being in the wrong place at the wrong time was when teaching a lad to drive, and he hit the rabbit. It was still alive, but I could not leave it in agony. Thankfully, he grew up on a farm, so he got out of the car and dealt with it.

We have had deer running out a few times, luckily, too far ahead of us to worry about. One time, we saw a rare albino deer running across the road, which was beautiful. However, deer may not be alone. It could be a herd, so be on the lookout as you approach.

Driving along another country road, two geese were waddling in front of us, one large, one small. The little one looked up to the big one as if saying,

"Where are we going?"

We had to slow down, unable to overtake because of approaching a bend. Even if there was no bend, the car behind was so close the driver would not have seen the geese. Fortunately, they waddled through the hedgerow back into the goose farm. They obviously fancied a walk!

Once, a peacock stood in the middle of the road, displaying its full plumage. Also, a swan flying towards the river miscalculated and landed in front of us on a bridge.

Cows had got out of a field, and again police were there, four of them. The cows were doing their own thing, going into people's gardens and chewing the flowers or running in the opposite direction of the officers. We had to sit and wait for them to clear the road enough to get through. Finally, the police got all the cows into someone's garden, so while the cows enjoyed the flowers, it was time for us to go. Sheep were on the road on another occasion. They thought the grass was greener on the other side of the fence. As they were on a country road and it was getting dark, I dialled 101 to let the police know.

A student's mother would pick up dead rabbits or pheasants killed on the road and take them home to cook. I do not know how you feel about that, but I felt sick. An old rule of the road is that the person who kills an animal or bird should not pick it up, but the person behind can! Yuck!

It was a hot summer's day lesson. We had parked on the left, with all the car windows open to keep us cool, and my door was slightly ajar. As I explained something to my pupil, five kittens came out of the garden next to us and got into my car.

"Oh, they're so sweet," Lisa said.

"Well, they're certainly making themselves at home here," I chuckled.

Two of them got onto the parcel shelf at the back of the car, and another two settled down on the rear seats, whilst the other one decided my lap was a good place to be.

"We'll just get on with the theory, then we'll have to get them out of the car and into the garden," I said as I stroked the one sitting on my lap.

Several times, cats and dogs have got into cars or vans and landed miles away from their homes because of a left open window, door or tailgate. So, check they are closed before you leave the vehicle.

My husband had to visit somebody who lived on a farm. This was before sat navs were the thing to have, and he was a little lost. He stopped to ask a person for directions to the farm, and the passenger door was open. They gave him directions and walked off. He was about to close the door when a Labrador jumped into the car.

"Hello," my husband said to him. "Want a lift, do you?"

The dog looked at him with the expression, "Well, drive on then!"

So, he carried on to the farm, and when he arrived, the farm owner came out to greet him.

"Oh," she said, laughing. "Thank you for bringing Toby back. He's always getting lifts off people coming up the lane." An astute dog!

I picked up a new lad and drove him to where I wanted to start the lesson. I parked up (we were on a quiet road), and as we swapped seats, we noticed a cat crossing the road. A few minutes later, we heard an awful screech of brakes. A car sped past us, breaking the speed limit and knocking the cat down. The cat had sat in the middle of the road!

We both got out of my car to see if it was still alive. It was breathing but badly injured. We were near where I lived, so I rang my house to see if my daughter was there as she once had worked at the local veterinary surgery. She came to us with a blanket and wrapped the cat up to take it to the surgery. As this was happening, the man who knocked the cat down came back but could not get around us as we were on the road dealing with it, and he had to stop. I thought I would not let him get away with this and went over to him.

I stormed at him. "If you had been driving at the proper speed limit, you would have had time to stop because you would have seen the cat ahead of you. To boot, nobody was behind you, and even if there was, you still would have had time to slow down and stop. You had children in the car. They saw what you did."

"I was late getting the children to a party, so I couldn't stop!" he replied.

"That's no excuse. You were speeding!" I retaliated. "A fine example to set before your children."

I made him give me his name, address and telephone number and told him I would knock on each person's door to see who owned the cat, and he would have to pay the vet's bill. I found the owner and learnt the cat was 20 years old. Sadly, it died. The owner was upset but thanked me for dealing with it and said they would make the driver pay his dues. Well, that was the end of the first lesson for this young lad, who was just as upset about it all as I was.

Some animals can mimic their counterparts. For example, while driving towards a zebra crossing, a cat sat at the kerb looking left and right. I told my pupil to slow down and stop before the crossing to see what would happen. The cat looked at us, checked the road again and calmly walked across the crossing to the other side of the road. You can imagine the oohing and ahhing from us in the car.

One evening while teaching my daughter to drive, we were on a single-track country road with a river running alongside it, and it was spawning time for toads. The toads were crossing the road to the river, and no toad crossing patrol operated that evening. So my daughter did the patrolling! She cleared seven or eight feet in front of us, then drove on to the next toad area, cleared that, and so on until we were free of them. Usually, it would have taken us around thirty minutes to get to the end of the road, but now it took us an hour. She was determined not to run over them. Good job for her, but I wondered what would have happened if a vehicle had been behind us!

Unhappily, in a lesson, two dogs ran out in front of us from a garden. We missed the first one but caught the back leg of the second one. Both dogs ran off, but we stopped and knocked on doors. However, nobody was at home. We then drove around to see if we could find them but to no avail. Hopefully, the dogs returned to their owners, especially the one with the injured leg, and they realised.

So, be careful when driving anywhere. Always be on your guard, as an animal could pop out in front of you anytime.

CHAPTER FOURTEEN

THE LAST CHAPTER

I did not think my career as a driving instructor would end as it did. I had a date set for retirement and was looking forward to my last few months of work, still taking pupils on but ensuring I had enough time to get them through their tests before I retired. However, there was a virus, COVID-19, lurking in our midst and little did we know the amount of havoc it would cause. A pandemic was on its way, changing people's lives dramatically, no matter who you were and suffering three lockdowns. The first lockdown came into force in England on 23rd March 2020. So, the DVSA cancelled driving lessons and tests, leaving instructors and pupils who had tests booked in a distressing situation.

I had three lads who were ready for their driving tests. Two of them had already taken a test but sadly failed. One of them had failed his first test in February 2020, and when we arrived at the test centre for his second test, the DVSA had cancelled it. They had sent him an email cancellation notice, but it had gone into his junk folder, and he did not see it. He booked the next test for 18th March 2020, and we ensured it was still happening. Still, when we arrived at the test centre, regrettably, his examiner was ill, and his test was cancelled. He was furious, and I had to calm him down. Not a pleasant ride home either! So, he had another date booked, but in July 2020.

The second lad kept putting off booking another test but finally booked it for 19th March 2020. However, he also got a cancellation notice from the DVSA, rebooking his test for July 2020.

The third lad needed help passing his theory test. So I started giving him theory lessons after failing his fourth test. He passed his fifth attempt and booked a practical test for July 2020.

The lockdown gradually eased at the beginning of June, and lessons could begin again on the 4th July 2020, and tests on the 22nd July 2020. However, the medical profession categorised my husband and I as clinically extremely vulnerable, so I was dubious about when to start teaching again. Even though all car cleaning would be done and masks would be worn, sitting next to somebody in such close quarters worried me. Also, there was the danger a person could unknowingly be a virus carrier and pass it on unwittingly. So, I had to decide whether to or not take the lads for their tests. I hummed and hawed, not wanting to let the lads down, but I had to make the painful decision not to and safeguard myself. Feeling gutted letting the lads know I could not take them for their tests due in July, I contacted another instructor who said he would take the three of them, for which I was grateful.

The virus was not subsiding with new variants arriving, causing more lockdowns. So, they imposed the second lockdown from the 5th November 2020 until the 2nd December 2020. Finally, the third lockdown started on the 6th January 2021, with a gradual easing from March until ending on the 21st July 2021. So, because of the lockdowns and my vulnerability, my last test was on the 8th February 2020. Finally, I retired in February 2021.

I have met many people with different backgrounds, personalities, and abilities. Teaching all my pupils (except the rude and cocky ones) was a pleasure. Some found it easy to learn and easy on my nerves. Still, I am incredibly proud to have taught those who overcame their hurdles and/or disabilities, even though it was hard work for them and me. They were determined to pass their theory and practical tests to give them the independence they needed.

Although I was a driving instructor for thirty-six years, I still worried about my pupils on the day of their theory and practical tests. I was sad they failed, but I still got a kick out of it when they passed.

If you want to learn to drive, have your full licence or become a driving instructor, I hope this book has given you food for thought.

Just one last thing about how being a driving instructor can drain your brain, as in the mishaps in the '*Petrol Station*s' chapter and on occasions where I have had brain seizures when I have gone to pick up pupils.

Once I got to know a pupil's pickup address, I did not write it down in my diary, just their name. However, they occasionally would ask me to pick them up from another area. But even though I would write the temporary address in my book, unfortunately, I still went to their usual address only to be told, "No, they're not here. Didn't they tell you to pick them up from……." Or there would be no answer, or I would be just about to knock or ring the doorbell and remember I should not be there. When mobile 'phones came in, it really helped, with a frantic text saying, "Sorry, going to be late."

However, once it was pretty embarrassing when I double-booked two girls who went to the same college. I turned onto the road where the college was, and one girl was standing on the corner. She waved, and I waved back, but I continued to drive up the road to where the other girl was, whose name I had written in my diary. It then dawned on me, as the girl at the bottom of the road started walking up towards me, that she was also waiting for me.

"Oh, flipping heck," I said to myself. "You've really gone and done it this time. You've gone and double-booked yourself!"

The girl from the bottom of the road reached my car. Both of them were standing there looking at me. I got out of the car and apologised to them for the mix-up, panic-stricken. I blamed it on the Tipp-Ex I used when I needed to blot out a name if they had cancelled a lesson, let it dry and then fill in another pupil's name. Obviously, this time, it did not go according to plan.

"What's going to happen now?" they both asked.

"I think we need to toss a coin and see who gets the lesson," I said.

"I won't charge whoever has the lesson today for the added inconvenience of driving the other one home, and she'll have another free lesson. The other girl will have a free lesson for missing today."

"That's not fair," one said, and the other nodded. "One of us will have a free lesson today and another one. Whereas the other girl will only have one free lesson."

"OK, OK," I said. "You'll both have two free lessons. One lesson for having to drive the other home, the other for missing today's lesson, and another free lesson each as an apology."

"Yeah, sounds good to us," they both said, nodding.

I can tell you I did not make that mistake again!

SAFE DRIVING OUT THERE!

ANECDOTES

From Various Driving Instructors' Pupils
(Each Given with the Driving Instructor's Permission)

Pupil: "Do ghosts have to press the button to cross the road?"

Instructor: "Nah, they're already dead, so you can hit them."

Pupil: "I didn't know the steering wheel turned."

Pupil: "Can I stop driving now. My arms are sore."

Pupil: "I'd hate to live down this road. The driveways are really close to the houses!"

Pupil: "Are these bumps on the steering wheel for blind people?"

Pupil: "Why do they have feet in miles?"

Pupil: "Why don't instructors have a steering wheel?"

Pupil: "Why is the car rolling backwards?" (She had stopped on the hill where she lived without the handbrake on!)

Pupil: "How am I going to reach the pedals over there?" (Looking at the instructor's pedals!)

Pupil: "If that t%*t behind gets any closer, I'm gonna get out and do him!"

Pupil: "Why is the car behind me getting closer?"
Instructor: "He's standing still. You're rolling back, you dick!"

Pupil: "Can you tell me why you're best to avoid large puddles?"
Instructor: "Because there might be animals in them!"
Pupil: "Really? What type of animals might we find?"

Pupil:	"In my previous instructor's car, gear 2 was at the top, and gear 1 was at the bottom!" (Pupil's excuse for repeatedly stalling and kangarooing down the road.)

Pupil:	"Has someone moved this seat?"
Instructor:	"Well, it may have been the other 17 learners who've been in the car before you!"

Pupil:	"What job do you do?" (Asking the instructor.)

Instructor:	As the pupil raised and lowered her seat, the instructor asked why.
Pupil:	"Because I can't see very well in the centre mirror!"

Instructor:	"Why did you get banned from driving?"
Pupil:	"Got caught with bald tyres!"
Instructor:	"What do you do for a living?"
Pupil:	"I work in a tyre garage!"

Pupil:	"How do you go straight on, and how do you signal?"

Pupil:	"How do you take the next left?"

Instructor:	"Try not to grab the steering wheel so hard when changing gear."
Pupil:	"Now you know why my husband left me!"

Pupil:	"If the lights are green, do I go?"

Pupil:	"I've been thinking about my crutch all week, and I'm going to make it smoother for you today!"
Instructor:	"Er, I think you mean the clutch!"

Pupil:	"Could you pass the driving test if you had to?" (Asking the instructor!)

Pupil:	"How do I know I'm at the give way line?"
Instructor:	"When you can see the white line under your door mirror."
Pupil:	"What's a door mirror?"

Pupil:	"Do I need to stop at a red light?"
Instructor:	"No, it's optional!"

Instructor:	(After a heavy day.) "Cark the par in a bay of your choice!"

Instructor:	(After a heavy day.) "Turn right at the thingmajigs, you know the whatchamacallits. Oh for @#%$! sake." (Instructor was trying to say traffic lights.)
Pupil:	(Approaching a red light.) "If it's green, do I go?"
Pupil:	"Can't believe how close that car is behind me, virtually up my arse!"
Instructor:	(At traffic lights as it starts to rain.) "Give the windscreen a wipe."
Pupil:	Went to get out of the car to wipe the windscreen!
Pupil:	(Asks what a sign means.)
Instructor:	"No stopping."
Pupil:	"What if the car in front of us stops at a roundabout!"
Pupil:	(After adjusting the mirror.) "Does that look OK to you?"
Pupil:	(After stalling.) "Did I do that?"

Instructor: (Points to a random pedestrian.) "No, it was him over there!"

Instructor: "How would you check the oil?"
Pupil: "I'd take this twig out and look at it!"

Pupil: "Where do we go at the over and about?"

Pupil: (Approaching a roundabout to turn right.)
Instructor: "Don't you think you should tell everyone you are turning right?"
Pupil: Pupil turns down her window and starts to shout to other vehicles she is turning right!

Pupil: (On her way to her third test.) "I've decided I'm having you on the back seat this afternoon!"
Instructor: "Er, really!"
Pupil: "Yep. It will be like I'm your puppet. Like you can make me do whatever you want, and I'll be able to feel you working me from behind!"

Pupil: (Accelerating towards a red light.)
Instructor: "Why are you accelerating?"
Pupil: "So I can stop!"

Instructor:	Asking the pupil what to expect along the country roads where there are a lot of horse livery yards.
Pupil:	"Er, rabbits, pheasants, cows."
Instructor:	"Something a little more domesticated."
Pupil:	"Goldfish."

Instructor:	"What road sign are we approaching?"
Pupil:	(After passing his theory test with full marks.) "Give me the options!"

Pupil:	"Why do we go faster downhill?"

Pupil:	"I'm steering round these puddles in case we sink!"

Pupil:	(Driving into a car park.) "What does I N stand for?"

Pupil:	"If you're gonna get up my arse at least pull my hair back!"

Instructor:	"What does that sign mean?"
Pupil:	"National insurance number!"

Examiner: "What would you be doing if you weren't on your test today?"

Pupil: (After telling the examiner his job.) "What do you do for a living?"

Examiner: (Replies in an amused way.) "Well, I'm a lorry driver!"

Instructor: "Tell me the next sign you see."

Pupil: "Pick your own strawberries!" (She wasn't wrong!)

Pupil: "What would happen if I hit a pigeon?"

Instructor: "It would probably die."

Pupil: "Would I go to prison?"

Instructor: (Asks a middle-aged woman.) "What are you up to after this lesson?"

Pupil: "I'm going home to give my husband a good time!"

ABOUT THE AUTHOR

Brenda Carey was a driving instructor for 36 years and is now retired.
She left school when she was 16 and became a junior secretary.
Eventually she worked her way up to become a personal assistant.
After eight years of being at home with her children, she wanted a change in career and driving instruction appealed to her. After passing the three tests, she taught for 36 years. Having in mind to write a book about her experiences, she began to make notes, and the result is 'Learner Driver on the Road'.

www.ingramcontent.com/pod-product-compliance
Lightning Source LLC
Chambersburg PA
CBHW070548050426
42450CB00011B/2772